How to Raise Disciplined and Happy Children

How to Raise Disciplined and Happy Children

Mastering the Power of Positive Reinforcement

Jerry Adams, Ph. D.

© 2011 Jerry Adams, Ph. D. All Rights Reserved

No part of this book may be reproduced, stored in a retrieval system, or transmitted by any means without the written permission of the author.

First published in June, 2011

ISBN: 978-1-463-53091-4

Printed in the United States of America

Cover art and design by Dan Adams, with contributions by Evan and Avery Adams

Typesetting by www.wordzworth.com

With eternal gratitude to my wife and parenting partner,

Julie Ann Adams,

*This book is dedicated to our sons,
their wives, and our grandchildren,*

and

To children everywhere . . .

*And to all who love, nurture, and guide them to become
responsible and caring members of society.*

Making the decision to have a child is momentous. It is to decide forever to have your heart go walking around outside your body.

–Elizabeth Stone

Table of Contents

Preface   vii

Introduction   ix

The introduction sets the stage for the rest of the book by identifying for whom it was written and by outlining what the reader will learn.

The Goal of this Book   x

How My Program Can Help You   xii

Chapter 1   Parental Disciplinary Practices and the Ways Children Learn   1

This chapter discusses serious limitations to common approaches to discipline, including the many counter-productive aspects of punishment. It highlights the various ways that children learn and how you as parents can use your understanding of how children respond to choose an effective approach. It then presents the framework for a comprehensive and coordinated approach to teaching children to behave responsibly.

Background   1

What Parents Say About Disciplining Their Children   2

Things We Know About Punishment   5

Ways Children Learn   8

Toward Establishing More Effective Discipline   11

Chapter 2   Power Struggles, Discipline, and Responsible Behavior   13

Chapter 2 recognizes the self-defeating results of power struggles between you and your children and describes what drives these destructive interactions, including the fearfulness that often

underlies a child's challenging behavior. And it prepares you for a constructive alternative that reduces any anxiety your child may experience, while ensuring harmonious parent-child interactions.

Observations on How Control Struggles Develop	14
The Way the Process Works	16
Resolving Power Struggles and Overall Discipline	18

Chapter 3   Exploit the Power of Positive Reinforcement   21

This chapter establishes the foundation for a structured proactive program focused on eliminating advantages to your children of their inappropriate behavior while assuring that they can meet their important needs by behaving responsibly. It also describes how you can eliminate already established inappropriate behavior without giving undue attention to inappropriate behavior.

Developmental Factors and the Learning Process	21
A Strategy for Constructive Discipline	23
Putting it Together: Summary of the Basic Rationale	32

Chapter 4   Three Steps to Develop a Custom-Made Home Program   35

Chapter 4 describes how to develop and operate a proactive home program to meet your family's specific needs. It spells out how to specify for your children the exact behavior you expect and how to avoid potential pitfalls that can undermine your program. Next it details how to establish a simple but powerful reinforcement program that makes it good for your child to comply with your expectations. Finally, the chapter discusses how to operate and monitor the program, using a simple behavioral chart and a brief but powerful daily reviews to assure ongoing constructive focus by all.

Step 1: Specify Your Expectations to Your Child	35

	Step 2: Help Your child want to do what you Expect	56
	Step 3: Build Your Program into Your Family Life	65

Chapter 5   Challenges in Developing a Home Program   75

To assist you in implementing the steps for constructing and implementing the home program discussed in Chapter 4, Chapter 5 presents a series of relevant questions from other parents about challenges arising in their homes. Illustrative examples are provided for each step.

	Step 1: Challenges in Specifying Expectations	75
	Step 2: Challenges in Establishing a Reward System	87
	Step 3: Challenges in Managing a Home Program	95

Chapter 6   Maintain the Program while Your Child Is Away from You   99

Chapter 6 describes how you can influence your children even while you are away from them, with specific attention to while they are at school.

	Step 1: Create a Partnership with the Teacher	100
	Step 2: Develop Shared Expectations	100
	Step 3: Develop a School Behavior Chart	102
	Step 4: Establish Operating Procedures for School	103

Chapter 7   How to Reduce Inappropriate Behavior   107

Since even the most compliant child sometimes misbehaves, Chapter 7 describes how to intervene without giving undue attention to unacceptable behavior. Since this powerful tool is so often misused, the pitfalls to avoid and the rationale for effective use of it are carefully discussed. Further, applications of the technique outside the home, specifically while at a sit-down restaurant, shopping, and in the car are discussed in detail.

	Misconceptions about A Powerful Tool	108
	How to Apply Time-out In Your Home	108
	How to Apply Time-out Outside Your Home	123
Chapter 8	**Monitor, Maintain, and Adjust Your Home Program.**	**137**

To assure long-term effectiveness, Chapter 8 discusses how to monitor and adjust the home program in response to faltering progress, to the child's mastery of behaviors, and to changing circumstances. Included are how to review, assess, and adjust the program. The chapter also includes a section on troubleshooting for times when the program appears stagnant.

	Review Progress and Adjust Your Program	138
	Adjust Your Program to Changing Circumstances	150
	Troubleshoot Your Program	155
Chapter 9	**Actual Families, Actual Challenges**	**159**

To further full mastery of this material, this last chapter presents a series of vignettes taken from my clinical work. Each addresses a question about how to manage specific aspects of developing, implementing, and operating a structured home program. My responses are intended both to address the specific questions raised and to illustrate how I think through the answers, to further your capacity to flexibly and effectively tailor the approach to your own families characteristics and needs.

Rewards or Bribery?	159
Learned Helplessness?	160
Focus on Self-initiated Responsibility	162
Managing Parental Stress	163
Managing Sibling Conflict	164
Differing Parental Expectations	165
When Saying "No" is too Difficult	166

When Your Child "Quits" the Program		167
Assisting a Child with Attention Deficit Disorder		170
Your Program and Children of Divorce		173
A Program for Parents, Too		176

Appendices 179

The three appendices are included to provide you with sample materials to support your efforts to build and operate your own home program. Each is explained at the beginning of the page.

Appendix 1	Identify Target Behaviors	181
Appendix 2	Blank Home Behavior Chart	185
Appendix 3	Sample Prize Game Board – Pre-Reading Age Child	187
Index		189

It is easier to build strong children than to repair broken men.

~Frederick Douglass

Preface

How to discipline children remains controversial, even in the 21st century. A few months ago an airline attendant reportedly took a 13-month-old baby from her mother after she was observed slapping the child's face. A storm of protest followed, fueled by those who asserted indignantly that parents are free to discipline as they see fit and by others who insisted that adults must take responsible action when they observe children being mistreated.

More recently, a mother seeking favorable reflection on herself, described her harsh demands for "perfection" from her children, in a book in which she claimed to speak for a whole culture of "tiger mothers." She summarily dismissed less demanding and controlling parents as lazy and proclaimed that "the solution to substandard performance is always to excoriate, punish, and shame the child." Surprisingly, these anecdotes and claims of one parent have generated heated and polarizing debate, one side extolling intense and strict demands on children and the other side repulsed by the belittling and demeaning methods propounded to meet those goals.

Responses to both the airplane incident and the new book reflect a distressingly misdirected focus on which is better: strict, demanding, punitive parenting or lax, laissez faire, child-placating parenting. In arguing the extremes, the discussion misses the most meaningful point: parents have constructive and effective alternatives and need not choose between leaving immature children to their own instincts and devices, on the one hand, and harsh, heavy-handed, and punitive reactions, on the other.

Fortunately, we have a rich body of knowledge supporting a positive and effective approach to encouraging the best in children, one that enhances their capacities to deal with their world as well as their sense of self-worth. The approach is based firmly upon the rigorously-demonstrated power of the Principle of Positive Reinforcement. Acting proactively, it is entirely possible for parents to provide guidance and direction to children learning to take responsibility for their own behavior, and to do so in a loving, carefully planned and managed manner that supports true success for all concerned. How much better it is for parents to learn suitable alternatives to teaching children appropriate behavior, to strengthen innate striving for mastery that is so characteristic of children, and to guide their maturation into capable, strong, and compassionate individuals.

Much of my professional life has been devoted to just that goal: helping parents help their children to assume age-appropriate responsibility for their own behavior. Over decades of facilitating classes for over a thousand parents, I learned a great deal about what is acceptable to parents and about what is effective, and I refined my approach accordingly. Parents attending the classes frequently suggested that I write a book to provide the course content in a concise and comprehensive form. In 2008 I attempted to fulfill those suggestions, in the form of *Discipline Without Anger: A Parent's Guide to Teaching Children Responsible Behavior*. This book met with modest success but readers suggested revisions intended to make the content more readily accessible for busy parents. *How to Raise Disciplined and Happy Children: Mastering the Power of Positive Reinforcement* is a result of efforts to make the best possible use of those suggestions. The new book is shorter by a good bit and is organized in a tighter format for easier use.

I am grateful to Carol E. Smith, M. S., Child and Family Therapist and Parent Educator, for her feedback and suggestions. I am profoundly grateful to Geraldine Kennedy, author and independent publisher, for the countless hours she spent revising and editing the manuscript; her probing questions and insightful comments provoked me to refinements I had never before considered. My older brother (a retired college English teacher), Lee, once again willingly provided careful reading and editing to improve the text, and his long-standing warm support has sustained me through many discouraging moments in the rewriting process. Our son, Dan, invested his considerable artistic talent and understanding of graphics design to produce the perfect cover for this book, as well as the game board shown in the appendix. Finally, Julie, my wife and a superb speech and language therapist with amazing insight into children and how to elicit the best from them, has continued to provide unstinting support and encouragement and cogent suggestions about ways to enhance the final revision. Anyone who gains from reading this book owes each of these people a special thanks.

Introduction

There is no entrance exam and no state certification is required. Becoming a parent is so easy that it often happens by accident. Yet raising children is the most profound undertaking of our lives. Prospective parents fantasize about calmly and tenderly guiding their new babies, carefully avoiding whatever mistakes they feel their own parents made with them.

In contrast, once they are actually parents, they are confronted with the daily realities of a needy and demanding infant and often find their patience short and their successes surprisingly limited. Bit by painful bit, they discover that true success in child-rearing does not come so easily and requires effectively managing a relentless procession of perplexing and ever-changing challenges.

How frustrating it is for parents, deeply committed to providing the best for their children, to be confronted with non-compliance and to find their interventions to be ineffective. Most are eager to provide loving guidance but when their children suddenly become stubbornly unresponsive, their own efforts as suddenly can feel highly ineffective.

Sadly, research shows that whenever unacceptable behavior proves persistent, the default response is likely to be more reliance on punishment, even though parents often acknowledge knowing this does not achieve lasting changes in their children's behavior.

As a Clinical Child Psychologist, I have devoted much of my attention to supporting parents who are working to help their children master the challenges of childhood and mature into responsible adults. Early on it became obvious that most modern parents have had little opportunity to learn fundamental principles of child development and what influences and changes behavior. As I worked with more and more families, it became clear that it is far easier and more effective to guide children to behave responsibly in the first place than it is to wait for them to behave inappropriately and then to punish them for their errors in hopes of bringing about lasting improvements in their behavior. In response, years ago I set about developing a class to provide parents (and all others who serve the parenting role) with a comprehensive approach to positive and effective discipline.

Review of extensive research on how behavior is established and what changes it led me to the most fundamental and widely accepted finding in all of psychology, education, and related fields. That finding, upon which I based the approach presented in my classes, is embodied in the powerful Principle of Positive Reinforcement, which states that:

> *Any behavior that occurs and is followed by a reinforcement is more likely to occur again.*

This simple statement carries with it profound and commonly misunderstood implications. Too often the power shows itself in inadvertent reinforcement of inappropriate behavior; when parents finally give in to their child's whining for a toy in the supermarket, the principle is at work in the form of reinforcement of behavior which is exactly opposite of the parents intentions. Indeed, both this child, smirking as he clutches his new toy, and another child beaming over praise earned for an "A" on an arithmetic test, are responding just as the principle predicts: they each are more likely to behave the same way again when similar circumstances arise.

It is crucial to understand that this Principle of Positive Reinforcement is a reality that exists in nature, whether or not we recognize that fact. It is no more a matter of conjecture or debate than is the direction of sunrise in the morning; rather, it is just the way it is. Thus, gaining mastery over this ever-present and profound influence on your children's behavior is essential to effective parenting.

How to Raise Disciplined and Happy Children: Mastering the Power of Positive Reinforcement is intended to guide parents to fully understand and effectively apply the principle. The rich accumulation of research on learning and behavior conducted over many years in clinics and laboratories around the world provides the underlying knowledge base which served as the foundation for my own clinical work and the classes I taught. My program is designed to help parents best apply the Principle of Positive Reinforcement to meet the needs of their families in their own homes, and ultimately to gain full mastery of its power to promote raising happy, responsible children.

THE GOAL OF THIS BOOK

How to Raise Disciplined and Happy Children is intended for parents who are committed to raising responsible children – parents (and all others who take on a parenting role) like you. The book is designed to provide you with an overall strategy for guiding your children to comply with your expectations and with those of the larger society. It is based on the conviction that children deserve loving guidance at each stage of their development, as they move from infancy, with its relative lack of responsibility; through middle-childhood, with growing expectations of cooperation; to adolescence, with ever-increasing demands and responsibilities.

My aim is to help you help your children learn to take appropriate responsibility for their own behavior. This goes beyond just helping you to better control your children to assuring that your children, in keeping with their ages and abilities, behave responsibly on their own, wherever they are,.

We teach two-year-old children to use the toilet. We teach kindergartners to take their turns during group activities. We teach fifth graders to sit quietly in class, complete homework, and respect their teachers. And, we certainly had better teach teenagers to be responsible for managing 3000 pounds of steel and glass at high speeds before we turn them loose to drive on busy highways.

Each of these is just a step in preparing our younger citizens to become caring, respectful, responsible, contributing members of our society, the ultimate goal of good parenting.

Please note that I am referring to children taking responsibility in the broadest sense of the term. This includes not only completing the usual chores and homework but also taking responsibility for how they relate to others, both their peers and adults, and for how they manage their own emotions. This is about learning to take control of their own lives and in the process to feel pride in their own accomplishments. Such learning does not happen overnight but rather represents an ongoing process which most of us continue throughout our lives.

> *Children are the living messages we send to a time we will not see.*
>
> ~Neil Postman

Children who behave responsibly typically receive strong positive reactions from others and if they receive enough such affirmations they come to feel capable and to act competently. In turn, when they feel competent, children are more willing to try new things, which results in new skills. When guided properly these steps yield still more responsible behavior and therefore still more positive feedback. This cycle represents a crucial support for children developing a pattern of success and maturation and ultimately forms a foundation for building strong self-esteem.

A lot has been written about the importance of building self-esteem in children by telling them how great they are, sometimes even in contexts where the children themselves recognize they haven't done so well. However, the evidence is pretty clear: the instances in which children observe and experience themselves succeeding are what really matter. Praise from others can support that process, but children must recognize that the praise is genuine for it to be effective. In fact, exaggerated flattery can backfire: children may conclude that they must be pretty pathetic for people to have to pretend they are doing okay when they know they are not.

How My Program Can Help You

The program described in this book will enable you:

1. To understand basic principles of human behavior relevant to what produces change in it. We will concentrate on the concepts central to how children learn to behave responsibly.

2. To grasp fully the significant differences between successful parenting practices and those that tend to inadvertently strengthen the very behaviors that most distress parents. You will learn to eliminate advantages to children of their inappropriate behaviors.

3. To understand the components of a carefully designed proactive program of behavior change for use in your own home.

4. To develop a list of target behaviors which define changes you want your child to master. You will learn how to select those behaviors you want to change, how to clearly and effectively convey your expectations to your child, and how to make suitable adjustments over time.

5. To design a system through which your child can meet important needs through responsible behavior, by defining a reward list tailored to your child's interests and your family's resources and by establishing a simple way to track successes and provide the rewards.

6. To create and implement a comprehensive program incorporating all of these elements, specifically tailored to achieve your family's goals.

7. To continue teaching your child to behave responsibly by extending your program and your influence into situations where you are not present.

8. To take calm and effective action on occasions when your child does behave unacceptably, whether at home or away, in a manner that respects all of the principles discussed here and thereby avoids new problems.

9. To monitor regularly and systematically how successful you are and to adjust your program as needed, based on your judgment of your child's progress and on changes in your child's responses to the program.

> *It's not only children who grow. Parents do too. As much as we watch to see what our children do with their lives, they are watching us to see what we do with ours. I can't tell my children to reach for the sun. All I can do is reach for it, myself.*
>
> ~Joyce Maynard

My intention is for you to understand all this so fully that you will be able to think through challenges in parenting as they arise and to have a clear basis for making whatever modifications become necessary over time. Over the years, I have had the pleasure of seeing parents rapidly master these concepts and practices, and I am confident that you can be just as successful.

This book was undertaken to capture my experience of working with a great many families over many years. To the extent that I have succeeded, the many parents with whom I worked deserve your thanks for their contributions to my understanding of how best to guide children to responsible behavior.

In order to give the concepts more vibrancy, I have included anecdotes throughout this book that illustrate common concerns and experiences of families working with this approach. To maintain the privacy of the families involved, each of these examples has been altered enough to hide actual identities while maintaining what is useful in each.

You have my best wishes for developing the proactive and positive parenting style most likely to get you and your family to your goals and for great joy as you watch your child blossom into a responsible, capable, confident individual who finds equal joy in mastering life's challenges.

If a child is to keep his inborn sense of wonder, he needs the companionship of at least one adult who can share it, rediscovering with him the joy, excitement and mystery of the world we live in.

–Rachel Carson

Chapter 1

Parental Disciplinary Practices and the Ways Children Learn

Background

"Children are to be seen and not heard." "Spare the rod and spoil the child." Such slogans have guided parenting across the ages and were thought by many to contain a great deal of wisdom and truth. Hidden from view was an ugly by-product of these views of children and how to deal with them: children from all social strata were being neglected and mistreated, emotionally and physically, by the parents upon whom they were dependant for everything.

Our society finally confronted this betrayal of the most fundamental trust only after a long struggle against laws that treated children as property. In the 1870's the American Society for Prevention of Cruelty to Animals successfully argued in court that children deserve protections at least as adequate as those provided to animals, and soon thereafter laws began appearing to limit the abuse of children at the hands of adults.

Over the centuries and across a great many cultures punishment was seen as the essential tool of discipline, to the point that the term discipline is commonly used as a synonym for punishment. This notion appears to be institutionalized in Western society:

> *In 2004 the British House of Lords defeated a law to outlaw spanking children even though adults aren't allowed to hit each other. A spokesman for Prime Minister Tony Blair stated, "The government wants an outcome that maintains the balance between the parent's right to discipline and protecting the child. That is why we don't want to criminalize parents. That is why we are opposed to outright bans. The government wants to send a signal that parents do have a right to discipline the child."*

In a similar vein in this county, proponents of corporal punishment commonly include the inference that discipline depends upon it. But to what extent does the focus on discipline through punishment represent the way that most modern parents deal with their own children?

WHAT PARENTS SAY ABOUT DISCIPLINING THEIR CHILDREN

APPROACHES PARENTS USE

Parents coming to the clinic where I practiced routinely completed a family questionnaire and some time ago I did a study of the answers related to my work. When asked, "How do you discipline your child," most parents responded that they used one or some combination of these three approaches:

Verbal Reprimands

Parents described cozy talks, lecturing, nagging, and out-and-out yelling to discipline their children. Verbal reprimands are common, but how effective parental talking is varies widely. Most parents experience occasions when all their instructions, counsel, and good advice seem not to be heard or heeded. All too frequently talking is simply non-productive and can even become counter-productive, especially when anger comes in to play.

Restrictions

Parents often respond to misbehavior by use of restrictions or by removal of privileges ranging from a few minutes in the corner to limits on television time to "grounding" for weeks, the severity varying both in degree of freedom and how long the limits last.

Taking away privileges appears to be a very common approach to discipline. Limiting privileges underlies the discipline in many schools, vaguely labeled "consequences" for inappropriate behavior.

Note that there is a profound difference between removing or withholding already assumed privileges and providing privileges only after a child has completed assigned responsibilities. When a parent takes away television time or use of a favorite toy, the child is likely to see this loss as "mean old dad and mom taking my stuff." On the other hand, when a child understands that responsible behavior is required before privileges are granted, the reaction is subtly but powerfully different. This standard teaches that restrictions of choices are based on the child's own prior choices. For example, a child who chooses not to complete homework on time is also choosing to forego the privilege of playing with friends for the afternoon.

Spanking

The third approach to discipline reported by parents was corporal punishment, ranging from a slap on the hand to swats on the behind, with some parents acknowledging pretty severe spankings.

> *If there is anything that we wish to change in the child, we should first examine it and see whether it is not something that could better be changed in ourselves.*
>
> –C.G. Jung

There are wide differences among parents as to whether they employ spanking as a form of discipline. While controversy continues to rage about whether it is essential or unnecessary, constructive or abusive, parents typically acknowledge little lasting benefit from its use.

What These Approaches Have In Common

These three approaches – verbal, restrictive, and physical (and combinations of them) – accounted for about 95 percent of parents approaches to discipline, the rest consisting of some form of praise and encouragement.

While the harshness of each approach can vary markedly, the three approaches also have a couple of key elements in common:

> All are applied only after a child has done something inappropriate (it would be strange to spank before a child does something wrong), and

> Since all represent a negative response to inappropriate behavior, generally they can accurately be considered punishment.

Reported Impact of These Approaches

The parents were also asked, "Does your approach get the results you are working for?" This question really asks: "Does punishment get the results you are working for?"

About 70 percent of the parents answered "no," indicating that they generally did not get the results hoped for.

Of the 30 percent who answered "yes" to this question, nearly all acknowledged that the changes they observed in response to punishment were only momentary and therefore their children did not show lasting improvements in their behavior.

Taken together, the results from this survey showed that very few of the parents felt that their attempts to teach responsible behavior through punishment were successful over the long run. This was true no matter what combination of verbal, restrictive, or physical approaches they relied on.

Many parents said that they had never considered discipline as related to responsible behavior. Instead they thought of discipline as the punishment they felt compelled to inflict when their children misbehaved. Given this level of reliance on punishment and its general ineffectiveness, it is important that we understand more about it.

PARENTAL DISCIPLINARY PRACTICES AND THE WAYS CHILDREN LEARN

Things We Know About Punishment

1. Punishment is best at teaching what not to do. If a child is pulling the cat's tail and you yell loudly enough or spank hard enough, the child will likely stop, at least for the moment. On the other hand, if a child is really resistant to doing homework, there may be no amount of yelling or nagging or spanking or grounding that will produce any serious effort whatsoever. Parents sometimes acknowledge becoming virtual prisoners in their own kitchens after insisting their child stay at the table until at least a few math problems are done. Punishment is typically ineffective in teaching children to do anything that they can avoid by stalling.

2. The effects of punishment don't last very long. Research shows that even though punishment may stop a behavior for the moment, it is unlikely that children really learn from it not to do the same thing later. Therefore, punishing children does not help parents achieve their goal of helping their children internalize responsible behavior.

> *Parents are not interested in justice; they are interested in quiet.*
>
> ~Bill Cosby

Bureau of Criminal Justice statistics show that over two-thirds of prison inmates are re-arrested within three years of release, and who knows how many of the other third simply are not caught for their repeated crimes? These facts provide further evidence of how truly ineffective punishment is as a means of teaching lasting responsible behavior.

3. Children who misbehave most benefit least from punishment. Children who typically do what is expected of them may respond to even mild chiding by quickly obeying and trying not to make the same mistake again.

On the other hand, children who repeatedly break family rules typically respond, even to harsh punishment, by continuing the same behavior. Some children actually challenge parents to punish them more, perhaps smirking as they do so. This can lead to a vicious cycle of misbehavior and increasingly harsh punishment as parents react to what appears to be complete disrespect and a direct challenge to their authority. When such children trust a therapist enough, they may admit that getting spanked hurts like the dickens and that they surely do not smile on the inside; they just are not about to let parents know how much it hurts and gain the upper hand. As a result, even more severe and more frequent punishment is unlikely to produce any real benefit and may even have a sizable detrimental effect.

4. When punishing, parents often lose sight of their goals. When parents react to unacceptable behavior by punishing, there is a very strong likelihood that in the process they will lose track of the original expectation. Sending a child to his room for failing to take out the trash may seem like a suitable response, but the trash sits where it was. Typically, focus on punishment distracts parents from the original responsibility, which falls by the wayside. I have known children who admitted preferring a slap to doing some detested task. It is important for parents to maintain their focus on the task at hand, realizing that side-tracking to punish may defeat both their intentions to assure the child completes the task and their longer term goals of teaching their child to be responsible.

5. Punishment injects anger into parent-child relationships. It is rare for parents to punish because they really want to; rather, they do so out of frustration at their lack of success with other forms of discipline. Similarly, children react to punishment with hurt and frustration, as well as with anxiety about disruption in parental love and support. If this joint distress is allowed to develop into a family norm, it may lead to deep-seated resentment and anger that can come to taint all parent-child interactions.

6. Punishment often actually increases behaviors it is meant to diminish. Frequently I have had a parent come into my office and say something like:

> *Joshua pinched his little sister hard enough to leave a red mark. I got so mad I spanked him until I felt bad myself. But, the next day he went back and did the same darn thing again! I sometimes wonder if something is wrong with the kid. I just know he knows better!*

If you think about it, the ideas that "something is wrong" with the child and that "I just know he knows better" are contradictory. Experience tells us that the parent is almost always correct in asserting that the child really does "know better." I have actually seen children, out of view of their parents, mouthing word for word what the parents were saying they had told the children at home. It is not that they don't know. And it is not that there is "something

PARENTAL DISCIPLINARY PRACTICES AND THE WAYS CHILDREN LEARN

wrong." I have treated individuals with severe disturbance, and I have never seen anyone disturbed enough not to attempt to avoid pain.

But then, why would the child do the same thing that just led to severe punishment? The answer is that there is something positive in it for the child, something gained, which is more important than avoiding the pain or inconvenience of the punishment.

Though parents typically don't notice it, whatever pain and inconvenience punishment causes for their children, they are always mixed with other factors that actually may work against their intended goal. These include the attention that the child receives from the parent who is doing the punishing.

> *The serious and chronic childhood illness of their ten-year-old son placed severe demands on the parents. In the middle of a family session, his otherwise quiet five-year-old brother suddenly asked, "Daddy, you know when I was little and always pitched fits at you?" Assured that his father remembered, the boy asked, "You know why I did that? I did it because then you would spank me. That way I knew I was part of the family." In this simple fashion, which brought tears to the eyes of the rest of us there, this little boy demonstrated how far children may go to meet their needs to be noticed and to feel important.*

In any interaction between parents and children, including those involving punishment, there may be other ways in which children's needs are met. Just as one example, a child who is caught up in intense sibling rivalry might well accept being punished along with the sibling in order to gain satisfaction from hurting the sibling who is seen as unfairly favored by the parent. This means that inappropriate behavior is reinforced even though reinforcing such behavior is exactly the opposite of the parents' best intentions.

7. When punishing, parents may cede control to their children. Child abuse is a serious problem in our society. Working in this field, though, I have always been struck by how really rare it is to come across parents who actually derive pleasure from abusing their children. Many parents who mistreat their children were abused as children themselves and act out of their frustrations because all they know how to do is react aggressively.

Think about what that means. When parents end up so frustrated with their children that they verge on abuse, the children are controlling the adults, rather than the other way around. Parents get into this situation not because they carefully plan it out but because they don't know what else to do. In that situation children may have a real sense of control or at least recognize the extra attention they receive. Thus, while parents take actions that they hope will stop behaviors they don't like, they end up instead reinforcing the very behaviors that they want their children not to do. Even parents who are not abusive but rely on punishment for discipline may unintentionally relinquish control to their children if they act contrary to their own values and standards.

Ways Children Learn

In reaction to harsh approaches to discipline, some parents in recent decades moved to the other extreme, allowing their children great freedom and expecting little from them. Now there is even professional training on how to treat the "over-indulged child syndrome," acknowledging concern that a good many children have had too few limits set on their behavior.

Ironically, both the get-tough and over-indulgent approaches fail in what is most basic to effective parenting. Evidence is clear that children do not fare well when they are raised harshly and without consideration of their developmental levels and emotional needs. At the same time, it is clear that children who are never taught that their behavior has consequences also do poorly.

> *Children are natural mimics who act like their parents despite every effort to teach them good manners.*
>
> ~Author Unknown

Too often the choice for parents seems to have been reduced to one extreme or the other. Even a great many people who claim that they use research-based approaches manage to align themselves with either end of the spectrum. For instance, schools may say that they use positive reinforcement principles but then rely on published lists of "consequences" consisting of prescribed punishments for various rule infractions.

A brief review of the ways children learn will provide some perspective.

Direct Instruction

Perhaps the most natural and common way to teach children is by directly telling them things, including what to do and how to do it. When your child was an infant, you began naming objects and saying things like "Wave bye-bye to Daddy"

PARENTAL DISCIPLINARY PRACTICES AND THE WAYS CHILDREN LEARN

while demonstrating. You have continued directly to instruct your child and someday you may even offer instructions on how to raise your grandchildren. (Of course, those of us who successfully use the principles and practices presented here will raise our children to be responsible adults. In turn, they are likely to use a similar approach in their own parenting. Isn't that a satisfying notion?)

CORRECTING ERRORS

Telling children what they have done wrong is a variation on direct instruction that comes very naturally to most of us. However, too much focus on mistakes can be damaging to a child's growth and development. Frequently being told how wrong we are eventually undermines how well we do all sorts of things. This is true whether we are children often scolded by our parents or adults often criticized by our supervisors.

MODELING

Adults typically laugh heartily while watching children play grownup, imitating our dress, speech, and actions in keeping with how they see us. Unfortunately, though, we often fail to notice when our children mimic some of our behaviors that we really don't like. The old admonition to "Do what I say, not what I do!" sounds good but almost always it is trumped by the more powerful reality that "Actions speak louder than words." As an example, I have had parents in my office complain that their teenager has taken up smoking, only to learn that the parents themselves directly model the behavior by smoking in the house.

In a somewhat different but related manner, parents sometimes encourage behaviors they really don't like by such actions as dressing their child in a shirt with "Little Devil" or some such across the front. Adults and children laughing at this little joke probably don't realize that they are directly reinforcing "devilish" behavior in the child who is basking in the glow of the laughter. Imagine how a child reacts to his parent's wearing a tee-shirt emblazoned with "I'm with Stupid" and an arrow pointing to the other parent. Surely the child will conclude from this that calling people such a name is cute and funny, not wrong – and parents may find respect for the "stupid" parent slipping as well.

The point here is that we parents constantly model behavior for our children, whether or not we notice, and the more we are aware of and choose to model the behaviors that we value, the more our children are likely to behave accordingly. Of course it is also important to assure that what we value is truly appropriate for our children.

Consequences of Behavior

In the last few decades, a lot has been written about the impact on children from the consequences of how they behave. In the 1960's many people allowed children to experience the **natural consequences** of their behavior, just as happens daily in the "real world." Unfortunately this whole idea led some parents to take a hands-off approach and "let children learn from their own mistakes." In some situations this may make sense, but carried to extremes, it can lead to real problems. As a clear, if rather grim example, imagine deciding that your child should learn not to run into a busy street by experiencing the natural consequence of doing so.

Recognizing such shortcomings, some child-development specialists recommend an alternative that they referred to as **logical consequences**. This approach relies on matching consequences to specific behaviors. It requires adults to guide children by showing them how their behavior causes problems and by choosing consequences to fit the problem. For example, a child hits a baseball and breaks a window. The logical consequence would depend upon the child's age. A five-year-old might be expected to hold the dustpan for the parent sweeping up the glass while a 16-year-old might be expected with supervision to buy and replace the glass. Here focus is not on criticizing the child but rather on the broken window and on the responsibility of those involved to make repairs. Blame is neither constructive nor necessary. While this approach has much to recommend it, one major drawback is that it typically involves waiting for a mistake to happen so that the child can learn from it.

> *If you want your children to improve, let them overhear the nice things you say about them to others.*
>
> –Haim Ginott

A more proactive approach involves **planning consequences** so that children are encouraged to behave appropriately in the first place, rather than waiting for them to misbehave and then reacting negatively in hopes of decreasing that behavior. For example, a mother aware that her seven-year-old daughter is struggling with arithmetic might tell her that when she completes five problems the two of them can take a break together and play for five minutes.

The concept of planning consequences for children's behavior, which also serve as the basis for my entire approach, is based on the following:

- To develop responsibly, children need and benefit from adult help.
- Waiting for failures to occur is not a very useful way to teach children to be responsible for themselves.
- Adult help can best be provided in a thoughtful, planned, proactive fashion that emphasizes the benefits of success.

Toward Establishing More Effective Discipline

To reach the goal of teaching children to take more complete responsibility for their own behavior, we must understand how responsibility is learned. Discipline is central to this process. Therefore it is essential that we start with a clear understanding of what discipline is and what it is not.

Throughout this book, **discipline** is understood to be the *process through which children **learn** to take **responsibility** for their own behavior.*

The emphasis here is not on what we do to children but rather on what happens **inside** them, so that they control and manage their own behavior.

Building on this conceptualization, we will establish a constructive and effective approach to discipline which:

- Respects the specific needs, attributes, and developmental levels of children;
- Accepts that it takes time and patience for children to learn what is appropriate and to comply with adult expectations;
- Acknowledges that adults are the ones to guide children to age-appropriate levels of responsibility for their own behavior; and
- Recognizes that teaching children that responsible behavior leads to beneficial consequences prepares them to function as effective members of society.

This approach lays a solid foundation for children to learn how the society actually works:

- People who are productive can expect benefit from their efforts: You do your part, and you get a payoff;

- People who cooperate with or help others are likely to receive thanks and praise: You take the needs of others seriously, and you get noticed and appreciated; and

- Generally no one gets paid in anticipation that they may someday do something productive: You don't benefit from making promises; you perform first and then benefit.

Whenever you see a boy whining incessantly for a toy in a store, you can be almost certain that he has gotten what he wanted by whining in the past. Children, just as is true for adults, strive to meet their own needs in whatever ways they can, doing what they sense will work. We must show them they can best meet their needs by doing what we consider appropriate so that they no longer have reason to misbehave.

Teaching responsible behavior requires the patience necessary to provide the time, effort, and focus central to true learning. Teaching discipline requires that we maintain discipline for ourselves, both with respect to understanding what we must do and with respect to doing it consistently. Be assured, however, that the approach presented in *How to Raise Disciplined and Happy Children* does not demand perfection! It is based on realistic responses from typical people working with typical children.

Over many years this approach has assisted many parents in guiding their children. No one did things perfectly. Those who succeeded did so by working day by day to be more effective, finding ways to succeed when progress bogged down and recovering from any slips into less constructive reactions. Just as we must forgive ourselves for our human inconsistencies, we must be prepared to understand and to forgive our children for theirs. Successful parents expect the same thing from themselves and from their children: do better tomorrow when things don't go perfectly today.

Chapter 2

Power Struggles, Discipline, and Responsible Behavior

Over years of working with parents who were struggling with their children's inappropriate behavior, I have observed frequent and intense battles of will between parents and their children. Typically all sides become trapped in combat that no one can either win or escape. Work with children in individual psychotherapy and observations of family interactions in joint sessions have clarified my understanding of the insidious dynamics. They reflect a subtle, unspoken, yet powerful pattern of interactions that tends to distort family relationships while operating outside of the awareness of those involved.

OBSERVATIONS ON HOW CONTROL STRUGGLES DEVELOP

1. The world is a scary place and children are not immune. Every newscast and every newspaper is filled with reports of burglaries, tornadoes, murders, wars, auto collisions, earthquakes, and the like. Clearly even very young children are exposed to a great many frightening experiences, including many we adults may not even be aware of.

> *An eight-year-old boy was treated on a pediatric ward for a bone infection, including weeks in traction with a pin in his knee and with continuous IV medication. He had been consistently delightful and cooperative with staff until the eve of having the pin removed so he could go home, when he became unruly and belligerent. Even his favorite nurse could not calm him, and the staff asked me to consult.*
>
> *Shrieks and curses guided me to the boy's room. He was in a rage, screaming complaints that revealed intense terror. Through his tears and distress he was able to tell me about the leg on his sister's doll falling off when the pin came out and his intense fear that the same thing was going to happen to him. Once he was reassured that his leg had healed and that he no longer needed the pin or traction, he relaxed, resuming his previous pleasant and cooperative manner.*

Many things cause fear in children, and fear of the unknown can be particularly distressing, especially when adults do not seem to see the danger or to understand and therefore don't offer much-needed support.

2. Children have few mechanisms for managing their fears. Adults commonly assume an intellectual distance between themselves and danger:

> *The shootings last night were far away in that bad part of town, or*
> *That hurricane was way out in New Orleans, or*
> *The terrorists will be caught and we'll be safe in our area.*

For most adults most of the time, these rational thoughts usually are sufficient to hold the world's threats at bay.

Children, on the other hand, are less able to rationalize away their concerns, instead seeing many threats as very personal. Children tend to be very concrete and to misjudge time and distance that may serve to comfort adults. Further, many children are, at best, inconsistently capable of separating fiction from reality. They may vividly remember frightening television programs long after viewing them, troubling their sleep for several nights. Further, they tend to mix things that they don't understand with what they do, often compounding their concerns.

> *During consultation on a pediatric ward, I met with a boy who had a tumor behind his left eyeball. Asked what "tumor" means, he told me he had a "tissue" behind his eye, a seemingly accurate and mature notion. Pursued just a bit more, however, I learned that the child imagined he had some sort of gunky, nasty, facial tissue wadded up and jammed into his head, somehow growing there. While the actual tumor was indeed a serious threat, what this boy imagined seemed more troubling to him than the more accurate description he was then given by his doctor.*

3. Children look to adults for protection and a sense of security, and, of course, parents are the first adults to whom most children turn.

Toddlers in a new situation can be observed venturing a bit away from their mothers' knees, only to rush back for reassurance when they get too far, a bolder child does something scary, or someone makes too loud a noise. As children grow older, they may use the same approach in different ways, for example wanting to sleep with the parents or asking for scholastically unneeded help with homework whenever they feel insecure.

> *Good, honest, hardheaded character is a function of the home. If the proper seed is sown there and properly nourished for a few years, it will not be easy for that plant to be uprooted.*
>
> ~George A. Dorsey

4. When children sense their parents cannot protect them, they become very insecure. Success in controlling parents leaves children feeling their parents must not be very strong and leaves them fearful about who will deal with all the threats in their environment. Because the experience of being in control can have such a profound impact on a child and on family interactions, it is important for parents to have a clear understanding of the implications. In general, the child is in control of adults whenever:

a   Parents wear down and give up in the face of their child's persistence; for instance after hours of repeated, "Please, Dad, can I, please, please, please?" the father finally reacts angrily with, "Oh, okay, but just this one time!" – perhaps for the hundredth time.

b   Parents change decisions they consider appropriate if they can't justify them to the child's satisfaction, for instance when "all the other children get to go" and Mom can't think of a good, compelling response to that.

c   Parents, against their better judgment, strike out at the child (physically or verbally) in frustration. Whenever parents react in ways that violate their own standards for dealing with a child they love, the parents are no longer in control of their emotions, of the child, or of the situation.

d   Parents react to child provocation in any other way that violates their own values or standards or otherwise is basically unacceptable to them.

The Way the Process Works

Whenever a child is in control of important adults (or perceives it to be that way, which amounts to the same thing), the child experiences a sequence of reactions:

1   First, the child experiences a brief but intense sense of satisfaction, powerful reinforcement for whatever behavior is occurring at the time, however inappropriate it might be. Sometimes children smirk in response, infuriating their parents who reason that if the child wins, then they have to lose.

2   Almost immediately after that first surge of satisfaction, the child recognizes a continuing dilemma, raising an unexpressed but troubling question:

   Gosh, if I am in control of Mom and Dad, who the heck is taking care of all the scary stuff out there?

Imagine being a child facing such a frightening dilemma. If you sense your parents are not capable of protecting you, you are left to protect yourself. How will you react? You will try to convince yourself that you are able to handle whatever scary things come along on your own. You are most likely to rely on what you know best how to do: whine more, fuss more, poke at your parents'

POWER STRUGGLES, DISCIPLINE, AND RESPONSIBLE BEHAVIOR

soft spots more, and keep up this pattern until they give in one more time. Success in that effort will demonstrate anew how strong you are and maybe that will allow you to feel safe.

Unfortunately, this attempt is doomed to fail. No matter how often you manage to control your parents, it remains clear you are still incapable of handling all the threats in the world. In our world no one is able to deal with all of the potential dangers and we must depend upon others. One of the cardinal features of maturity is the capacity to accept that none of us is strong enough to handle everything and that we must and do depend upon others to survive. In our world we cannot have milk without depending upon – and trusting – perhaps a dozen people between the cow and us, all of whom have to do the right thing for the milk to be safe. Yet, because generally we are able to trust others, we drink milk and rarely think about the many points at which it could be contaminated.

But a child who feels in control of adults does not dare to feel trust for anyone or anything, a burden of almost unimaginable magnitude. Given the extent of children's dependence on adults for protection, the intensity of this quandary can hardly be overstated. Such a pattern may provide the basis for much bullying behavior, seen in children working to convince themselves they are not as vulnerable as they feel inside.

In sum, in response to this dilemma, the child struggles to feel strong enough by testing the adults' and the child's own resources, that is, by pushing the limits of inappropriate behavior. Of course no child will consciously think this all through; it remains outside conscious awareness, rather than a conscious decision of how to react.

3. The most common response from parents, when their children test the limits, is increased frustration followed, as for the children, by doing more of whatever they did earlier (e.g., giving in, wearing down, or striking out). Because of the intense feelings involved, any such responses are not well thought out and are expressed harshly enough to provide still more evidence that the child is stuck in control. That realization, in turn leads the child to renewed worries and fears about being in control, continuing the entire process.

4. All of this results in a vicious cycle that reflects the common experience of families caught in such patterns:
    - The more the child feels in control . . .
    - The more apprehensive and fearful the child is . . .

- The more the child challenges the limits with unacceptable behavior...
- The more the parents react angrily and ineffectively . . .
- The more the child's sense of being in control is confirmed . . .
- The more likely the entire process will continue to repeat itself.

On the one hand, then, we have a child who tries the parent's patience, who brazenly challenges every rule, and who tempts the parent to react harshly, thereby leaving the child in control. On the other hand, that tiresome, challenging, frustrating child is, in fact, frightened, apprehensive, and struggling to allay fears by acting as if able to control whatever scary things come along.

Resolving Power Struggles and Overall Discipline

Caught in this dilemma and with no understanding of what is happening, the child cannot resolve the dilemma.

Rather, it is up to adults to overcome their frustration and find a loving way to respond in order to calm the child's fears and eliminate the struggle.

> *A parent who has never apologized to his children is a monster. If he's always apologizing, his children are monsters.*
>
> ~Mignon McLaughlin

Ironically and sadly, it is precisely at these times when a parent feels least nurturing that the child caught in a control struggle most desperately needs comforting. Once parents understand that the child is reacting out of fear and apprehension even though the behavior appears cocky and disrespectful, their challenge is to regain and maintain control, providing security and safety through well-defined limits on the child's behavior. Accomplishing this will demonstrate strength that is not threatening to the already anxious and apprehensive child, the strength that will keep the child and the family safe.

But how can parents achieve this goal? Parents in my classes volunteered a couple of possible ways to deal with this challenge.

Some parents asserted that "If the little so-and-so needs to see strength, I'll show him strength," typically said with one fist aggressively slamming into the opposite hand. As understandable as that reaction seems at first, it is unlikely that a threatening stance can provide the reassurance so deeply needed by a frightened child. In practice parents almost never react punitively based on their own controlled and reasoned reaction, but rather they react to – and therefore remain controlled by – their child's reactions.

Other parents suggested that "If Tyler would just quit testing me all the time, he'd see I am here to take care of him and his needs." This, too, seems like a perfectly reasonable idea until we look closer at it. First, this assertion suggests that Tyler delegate authority to the parent and it is clear that a person delegating responsibility remains in charge. (As President Truman put it, "The buck stops here.") Second, for Tyler to back off so that his parents can exhibit their strengths, he would have to trust that his parents can handle things, but inability to trust in that fashion is the root cause of the problem in the first place.

So if reacting harshly or waiting for the child to relinquish control is not the solution, what is? First the parents must be very clear that their goal is to:

- Establish clear boundaries between what the child can and cannot control, that is, set appropriate limits, and
- Enforce, consistently and effectively, those boundaries; no must mean no, both when it is said and when it is challenged.

The idea is to show the child that the boundaries are there, that they are firm, and that the limits themselves can be relied on to provide protection.

> *You and three-year-old Paul live in a house with nothing but a few feet of grass and the sidewalk between your front door and a very busy street. Paul wants to explore out the front door, but you know that you must set clear and firm limits. You recognize that confining Paul to the house assures his safety but also severely limits his opportunities to learn about and deal with the larger world and thereby gradually to become more independent. To avoid stifling his growth, you install a fence to keep Paul safe while also giving him greater freedom. You recognize that Paul could fall and hurt himself in a fenced yard so that you have not protected him against all mishaps but you know that the fence balances freedom to expand horizons with safety from what could be a very major injury.*

Children need their parents to establish clear boundaries:

> *Within which they are free safely to learn about the world and Beyond which they cannot venture. Period.*

I recognize that most parents already accept these as ideals and typically have tried valiantly to achieve them, often without much success. Fortunately, once we have a clear understanding of the dynamics operating in such situations, it is possible – and not as difficult as parents often fear it will be – to establish a parenting style and approach that will assure that children adhere to limits set by parents. And, when that happens, even children with long histories of challenging behavior are relieved from the anxiety that drove them earlier.

In sum, avoiding power struggles by consistently setting and enforcing suitable limits is central to raising happy and responsible children. Since reliance on punishment increases the likelihood of sliding into power struggles in the first place, it is essential to keep these important points about punishment in mind:

- Punishment is best at teaching what not to do.
- Even then, the effects of punishment tend not to be lasting.
- Punishment is more likely to be effective with children who least need outside help to become responsible.
- Punishment serves to distract parents and causes unnecessary and counter-productive anger and frustration in parent-child relationships.
- To make things worse, punishment often works against the intended goal by providing attention, a sense of control, and/or other counter-productive benefits, thereby inadvertently reinforcing the very behaviors parents want to eliminate.

In conclusion, punishment generally is ineffective and often actually interferes with teaching responsible behavior.

Chapter 3

Exploit the Power of Positive Reinforcement

Developmental Factors and the Learning Process

Picture your child as a baby just a few days old. Several times every day your baby gets hungry, and, as babies do, cries. When you pop some milk into the baby's mouth, the crying stops, replaced by sucking. This very clear change in behavior, based on a natural, instinctual reaction, can be referred to as **a response to "material" reinforcement**. While this is so natural that hardly anyone pays much attention to it, it is the very important first stage of a lifelong pattern of responding when provided "stuff," continuing later as responses to such things as cookies and, later yet, to pay checks.

Now picture the same baby, three or four months later. The baby gets hungry and cries, just as before. But now when the baby spies mom hustling into view, typically the crying stops even before any food is provided, replaced by sucking motions, babbling, smiling, and flailing of arms and legs. While this change in behavior, not seen in the newborn, will not last long for a hungry baby, it is the beginning of another important, lifelong pattern, **a response to social reinforcement**. Almost always at first the response is seen in reaction to mothers, but typically it generalizes, carries over, pretty quickly to fathers, siblings, grandparents, and others who are close at hand.

What is so fascinating about this development is that within a very few weeks after birth your child's behavior matures from innate and instinctual to learned. What once depended on satisfying hunger through milk now occurs because the mother, who has become associated with the milk, appears. This provides solid evidence of the capacity of even such young babies to learn and equally solid evidence that parents have a significant and direct impact on their child's behavior. Knowing that you have so much influence should be very exciting – and perhaps sobering – to you as parents.

Responses to material reinforcement and to social reinforcement are two steps along the way to the third and final level, when the child has come to **respond to internal reinforcement**. This can also be seen as the goal of parenting, the stage in which the child has learned to take responsibility.

It is more difficult early in life to identify a perfect example of this third level but a couple of illustrations will serve to clarify the idea.

> *Picture your child, not yet walking but pulled up and holding on to a low table. The child sees a red ball out of reach a few feet away on the sofa. Dropping to crawl toward the ball, the child will lose track and never reach it. But the first time the child lets loose of the table, takes those few steps, and reaches the sofa, two wonderful things happen. First, by reaching the ball the child immediately achieves the material reinforcement. And second, observing parents fill the air with squeals of delight at those steps, thereby providing intense social reinforcement. With each repetition of the act which is followed by material and social reinforcement, the child's proficiency in walking grows.*
>
> *While it is true that there is a physiological maturational aspect of this process, when and how well the child moves through the learning process depends upon the payoff that the behavior elicits. The impact is so powerful that a few weeks later the child will be motoring around smoothly and confidently, leaving behind those clumsy first steps.*

Another, admittedly odd, example has been helpful to parents in my classes.

> *Imagine a toddler who is well toilet-trained by two and a half or three years of age. Then imagine asking the child, at age five or six, to wet his*

> *or her pants. (No, I haven't ever actually done this!) Chances are you couldn't get so much as a drop, even if you asked many children. The reason is that, by five or six, children who were toilet trained by age three have so fully internalized their behavior that it is as if they are reinforcing themselves for using the toilet properly.*

This odd example can be extended to the adult world:

> *Imagine yourself at a conference attended by a thousand people crammed into a large meeting room. On the way in, you all had breakfast with juice and coffee and everyone is seated at narrow tables containing tumblers and ice water. The room is stuffy and warm, the meeting long, and a lot of water is consumed. Within an hour or so, a lot of people are squirming in their seats. The lucky few seated near aisles slip out, gain some relief, and return, but you and the vast majority are left to sit in growing discomfort.*
>
> *Now ask yourself: how likely are you during this experience to think, "Gee, this is so uncomfortable that I'm just going to let it go!" Probably none of the hundreds of adults sitting in considerable distress would even think of that simple solution. This is the end result of the process of internalizing reinforcement for relieving ones bladder only in certain places and at the right times, long after receiving material and social reinforcement for just that restraint during toddler-hood.*

A Strategy for Constructive Discipline

How can parents take advantage of the natural developmental influences on children's behavior to construct an effective approach to discipline?

The answer involves a strategy for discipline with two equally important components, both direct reflections of the power of positive reinforcement.

Eliminate the Advantages of Inappropriate Behavior

The first component of our strategy requires *eliminating the advantages to children of their inappropriate behavior*, withholding attention, a sense of control, and all other benefits when children behave inappropriately.

The concept to keep clear in your mind and to come back to any time you are in doubt is this:

> *To the extent possible, **ignore** behaviors you consider inappropriate.*

If you read that statement with apprehension or disbelief, you are not alone. Often parents' instincts tell them that if they dare to follow this guide, their children will go wild. The reassuring thing is that those instincts are almost certainly correct; if parents *only* do this part, it will likely make things worse, even much worse, at least for a time.

> *An educational specialist was asked to observe in class a boy whose behavior distressed his teacher and his parents. He was described as a class clown, constantly doing cute things that in the classroom caused problems, including eliciting giggles from the other children. Between the referral and the consultant's arrival, the teacher had decided that the child was responding to attention from his classmates, and she decided to deal with that fact directly.*
>
> *When the consultant arrived, she observed a surprising scene. The teacher was in front of the class with all of her pupils paying close attention to her, except for the little clown who was out of control, running around the room, crawling under desks, and making weird sounds. The distraught teacher admitted giving serious consideration to burning whatever book had suggested this approach.*

Despite her dismay at the result, the teacher likely was right in thinking that the child misbehaved for attention from his classmates. Unfortunately, her solution of simply removing the attention the child so enjoyed failed to address the need for attention that drove the child's behavior in the first place. If the child had been behaving in such fashion because of a desperate thirst, surely the teacher would not have withheld water while expecting a reduction in struggles to get the water. Similarly, withholding attention from the class clown served directly to increase his need. In response, the child did what we should expect in order to meet those needs: he intensified the behavior that had met his needs previously, namely his clowning.

In theory, what the teacher attempted was a possible solution to the problem.

It is well known from research that if reinforcement of a behavior is discontinued, then eventually the behavior can be expected to "extinguish," that is, to no longer occur. However, in a classroom full of active children, it would be impossible to assure that the child never was reinforced again. Even occasional attention, such as one child giggling, would be enough to keep the behavior going. As a result, attempting to extinguish the behavior would just frustrate the teacher and would impose a heavy burden on classmates expected to ignore the clown. Further, this approach would be very hard on the boy himself. He would have to live through a long, unsuccessful struggle to meet his need for attention and to feel important to others, all the while feeling bad about his misbehavior.

> *Children aren't happy with nothing to ignore*
> *And that's what parents were created for.*
>
> —Ogden Nash

Fortunately it is not necessary to put any of the players through such a difficult sequence. What is needed, instead, is to understand that while the teacher's approach had merit, it failed to provide the child with a workable alternative way to meet his needs. That is, she did not provide the child a way to gain attention without clowning around during class.

Provide Advantages for Responsible Behavior

During a typical day parents are likely to reward their child's appropriate behaviors numerous times, often without any thought or even awareness. By consciously thinking about the processes involved and by arranging their responses to their children accordingly, parents can bring to bear the full power of positive reinforcement as they teach their children to behave in the way the parents consider appropriate. In the process children learn to internalize those patterns of behavior so that they become their own. That is the basis for our approach:

> *Consistently responding positively to appropriate behaviors while consistently withholding response to inappropriate behaviors produces lasting, internal maturation in our children's behavior.*

Thus, we have worked our way back to the fundamental principle expressed previously and underlying our strategy for raising happy, responsible children:

The **Principle of Positive Reinforcement** – probably the most widely demonstrated and fully accepted principle in all of psychology, education, and related fields of study – states that:

> ***Any*** *behavior that **occurs** and is followed by **reinforcement** is **more likely** to occur again.*

I was introduced to this principle early in graduate school and could cite many studies on which it was based. Still, only when I began working with families using this approach did I fully appreciate the principle's profound implications and its full power. What follows is intended to assure you won't experience a similarly delayed understanding

First, the principle refers to any behavior, whether the behavior is appropriate and desirable or just the opposite. We all were taught that "practice makes perfect," but as you strive to guide your children to responsible behavior, keep this more accurate notion in mind: "practice makes permanent." As the Principle of Positive Reinforcement states, *any* behavior that is practiced enough will become a habit, and whether it is "perfect" depends entirely upon how the behavior is viewed. That is, the principle is neutral with respect to the type of behavior so that literally any behavior is covered, even when you may not realize that the process is operating.

> *You are talking to a friend on the telephone, fully engrossed in an enjoyable conversation, unaware that your little girl across the room is drawing on the wall with crayons. Meanwhile, she is watching you, equally unaware that your responses have nothing to do with her and she may well be reinforced for drawing on the wall simply by hearing your laughter at your friend's comments.*

Here, unrelated to any intention on your part, by observing your amusement your child's behavior is directly reinforced, so that she is more likely to repeat the behavior than if she had not seen your smiles. Further, even when you are aware of what is happening, it is possible to unintentionally reinforce a behavior, sometimes to your own dismay.

> *As I discussed their concerns with his parents, a small boy explored my office, which is typical behavior for children in a new setting. Just as we three adults were laughing at the father's funny comment, we heard the sound of ripping paper. Still smiling, we all turned to the sound to discover the boy tearing a page from one of my favorite books. Despite ourselves and absolutely unintentionally, at that moment our smiles directly reinforced the behavior of tearing pages out of books.*

Since any and all behavior is subject to the principle, it is important that you consciously avoid inadvertently reinforcing behaviors you consider inappropriate for your children. To the extent possible, ignore behavior you would like to eliminate and reinforce behavior that you would like to encourage.

EXPLOIT THE POWER OF POSITIVE REINFORCEMENT

Second, the behavior must actually occur. Parents often are discouraged when they consider all the times their kids have resisted certain expected behaviors. Based on their experience that they can never get their children to do what they want, they are left wondering how this whole idea can help. Fortunately, being aware of all elements of the principle provides means of overcoming this concern.

Third, the behavior must be reinforced, which means that what follows must be positive and meaningful to the child in order for a behavior to become more likely. For example, a trip to an amusement park might seem like an effective reward but for a child who isn't interested, the offer does not provide any reinforcement value.

Fourth, reinforcing the behavior *increases the likelihood* that the behavior will occur again, but it does not guarantee it. Making lasting changes in a behavior requires a sustained period of reinforcement to assure the behavior will become internalized and therefore will continue to occur.

Thus, it is critically important to understand the "likelihood" notion. The simple scale shown here shows the impact of additional reinforcement on the likelihood or probability that a behavior will occur again.

Increased likelihood that a behavior will occur when a child is reinforced (rewarded)

100% probability (certain to occur)

x^2

x^1

0% probability (certain not to occur)

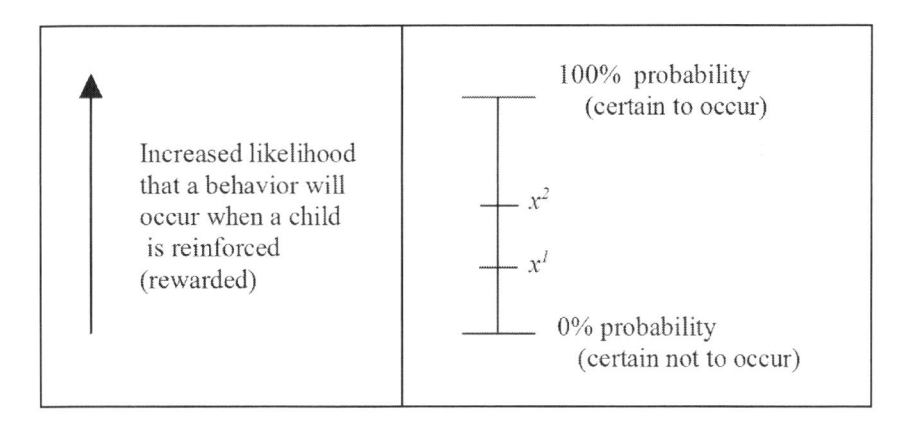

Figure 1. The probability of a behavior occurring increases with reinforcement

The line on the left shows that the probability or likelihood of a behavior increases whenever it is reinforced. On the right, the scale ranges from certain not to occur (0 percent probability), to certain to occur (100 percent).

Because Johnny sometimes takes the trash out and sometimes doesn't, we know he is able to do the task but hasn't yet taken responsibility for it. Also, because he does it sometimes but not all the time, we know that the probability he will do it is above zero but below 100 percent. Since we have no way to determine exactly where on the probability scale his behavior lies, I have placed a line at x^1 percent probability just to indicate a starting point.

The Principle of Positive Reinforcement tells us that if Johnny takes the trash out again sometime and is reinforced, the probability that he will do it again will go up by some amount. This is indicated on the scale by x^2, after being rewarded. Note that even though there is no way to know exactly how much change occurred, it is clear that some did occur.

Fifth, any success is important but does not guarantee lasting changes. Parents sometimes report trying a reward program of some sort – chip system, point system, or whatever – and finding that the program "didn't work." When describing those experiences, parents typically say that:

They tried the approach for a time,
The child seemed to do better,
They began to take the changes for granted,
They less and less often remembered to provide promised rewards, and
The behavior went back to the way it was or even got worse.

Our simple probability chart anticipates just such a development, indicating that if you stop this approach too soon, your child's behavior will revert to whatever you saw before you started. Increasing the probability that your child will do a certain thing as directed is important, but:

You must continue the reinforcement until your child is operating on the basis of internalized reinforcement.

Thus, reinforcing Johnny's success in getting the trash out does not mean he will ever do it again, but it does mean he is more likely to.

It is critical – and exciting – to realize is that if his parents can arrange for Johnny to take the trash out enough times and reinforce him enough times, they can count on his behavior to become internally reinforced, our goal.

It is useful to remind ourselves here that since the principle is neutral with respect to the type of behavior, all these points apply equally forcefully to behaviors you might not like.

Finally, remember that just as we have no way to determine how likely a child is to do a certain task, we also lack any gauge as to how many more times a child must be reinforced to internalize the reinforcement. This is inconvenient, but in practice it turns out not to be a big deal.

Eliminate Already Established Inappropriate Behaviors

The Bad News

Many parents say their children keep doing things they really dislike despite many efforts to stop them. The Principle of Positive Reinforcement, recognizing that **any** behavior which is reinforced enough times becomes internalized, offers a clear explanation. Almost certainly these children have been reinforced unintentionally many times for the disliked behaviors.

Parents who dislike whining often give in to their child to get the whining to stop, and in the process they teach the child that whining works, no matter how often they have heard it condemned. Actions really do speak louder than words, and when the child meets important needs while whining, the response carries the day no matter what the parents say about the matter.

> *While we try to teach our children all about life, Our children teach us what life is all about.*
>
> ~Angela Schwindt

What makes this dysfunctional interchange all the more insidious is that it works both ways. When parents finally get fed up and give in to the whining, the resulting peace and quiet provide instant, strong reinforcement for the parents' response of giving in. As a result, the likelihood the parents will give in the next time also increases. This powerful reality and the subtle nature of how it works explain how it is that parents tend to repeat their part in a pattern they so dislike.

The observation that children may internalize inappropriate behavior due to enough inadvertent reinforcement highlights a significant problem. Once a behavior is truly internalized, it is very difficult to dislodge. Psychologists, if they are fully candid, might acknowledge that we really don't know any *direct* and consistently effective way to eliminate inappropriate behaviors that are fully established.

That is the bad news.

The Good News

The good news, on the other hand, is that through careful application of the Principle of Positive Reinforcement, it is possible to overcome this potential roadblock, while bypassing any direct assault on the behavior. You can do so by identifying and selectively strengthening behaviors that you consider appropriate alternatives to those you consider inappropriate.

To eliminate ingrained undesirable behaviors, start by applying the first rule of our overall strategy: *ignore the behavior to be ended*; failure to follow this rule will undermine any other efforts you make. Then prepare to apply the second rule: *arrange for your child to meet his or her important needs by behaving appropriately.*

Specifically, focus your efforts on replacing the undesirable behavior with an alternative behavior that is both:

1   *Desirable and*
2   *Directly incompatible with the undesirable behavior*, that is, a behavior which, when it is occurring, will prevent the other behavior from occurring.

> *A third-grade boy disrupted his classroom by a variety of unacceptable acts, including running around the room, making lots of noise, and sometimes even pulling the hair of a girl in the back of the room. None of the teacher's attempts at discipline helped, including keeping the boy in at recess, moving his desk next to hers, having him write that he should behave, lecturing him, sending him to the principal's office, and contacting his parents. Over time the problem seemed to get worse.*
>
> *Finally the teacher called in a school psychologist, who unobtrusively observed the child for a while and then took him aside to talk with him. When the psychologist left, the boy was sitting at his desk right next to the teacher's desk where he mostly stayed during class from then on.*

Why the change? The specific steps taken were less dramatic than might be expected. The psychologist designed and taped to the child's desk a simple chart on which the child was to mark every ten minutes that he was seated at his desk. The teacher monitored the checkmarks to verify the accuracy. And the parents were asked to provide a material reward of some sort for a certain number of checkmarks. All of that is fairly straightforward.

EXPLOIT THE POWER OF POSITIVE REINFORCEMENT

What is missing from that description and what matters most here is the psychologist's reasoning process. What he asked himself was:

What is it that the teacher wants the child **to do** *which is* **also directly incompatible** *with the behavior she wants him* **not to do***?*

Clearly she wanted him not to run around the room causing problems, and particularly not to pull the hair of the girl sitting in the back of the room. What she *did want* was for him to sit at his desk. Clearly he could not run around the room and pull the hair of the girl in the back of the room while sitting at his desk. The psychologist focused the behavioral program on rewarding the child for sitting at his desk, through positive attention from his teacher and parents and some sort of material reward from his parents. This strategy also indirectly but effectively stopped him from wandering around and stopped his aggressive behavior elsewhere in the classroom.

I recognize that this simple but elegant solution has limitations. There is no guarantee that this boy will stay quiet and pay attention while sitting at his desk, though sitting close to the teacher improved the odds since she also was serving as part of the reinforcement chain. A more complete resolution of this situation likely would require more effort and planning. Still, eliminating a major part of the problem was a great start – as the girl whose hair was no longer pulled would likely attest – and clearly demonstrated that the child was amenable to change with appropriately targeted reinforcement.

Let's consider another example. Suppose ten-year-old Jessica picks on her seven-year-old brother Kevin. Among other things, she tells him, "You can't do anything right," and she calls him "stupid." All your efforts to convince her it isn't nice to talk like that to a brother she really loves, to ground her so she'll stop, and to swat her on the behind to get her to quit have failed to produce any lasting change. It is pretty clear what behavior you would want Jessica to stop doing. But what would you want her to do that is also directly incompatible with what you want her to stop? Here is one possible answer in the form of a target for behavior change that Jessica's parents could focus on:

Jessica, you are successful when you pleasantly help Kevin learn one set of his addition flash cards well enough to get at least eight of ten correct when tested by Mom or Dad.

You may come up with many other ideas about how to approach this. In this example, Jessica must stay pleasant and must actually help her brother accomplish something, a style that is incompatible with her taunts that he can't do anything right. Here the success behavior provides Jessica incentive to support

Kevin's successes and might well also instill some pride, both in herself and in her brother. Whether this item will be effective will depend in part on whether expecting Jessica to help Kevin get eight of ten items right is realistic and also depends upon the adequacy of the reward Jessica can earn for her efforts, both features under the parents' control.

> *In the final analysis it is not what you do for your children but what you have taught them to do for themselves that will make them successful human beings.*
>
> ~Ann Landers

As these examples show, the good news completely outweighs the bad.

Putting it Together: Summary of the Basic Rationale

Our goal is to teach children to take adequate responsibility for their own behavior so that as they move from infancy toward adulthood they become increasingly capable of handling the freedom and choice allowed them.

The most commonly used tools of discipline – verbal reprimands, restrictions, and spanking – generally fail to change children's behavior for the better over the long run and they may even make things worse.

To overcome these limitations we focus on two equally important components:

First, **eliminate** the advantages to your children of their inappropriate behaviors, that is, *ignore inappropriate behavior* and otherwise assure there are no secondary benefits from misbehaving.

Second, *proactively arrange for your children to meet their important needs through responsible behavior that assures them your positive attention and whatever material reward you have agreed to.*

Fulfilling these steps involves:

- Consciously taking advantage of the natural developmental progression over which you have considerable control, *selectively providing material and social reinforcement for behaviors you choose to increase*, and

EXPLOIT THE POWER OF POSITIVE REINFORCEMENT

- *Continuing to reinforce those appropriate behaviors long enough to assure your children come to independently reinforce themselves.*

Fundamental to this approach is the Principle of Positive Reinforcement: that *any behavior that occurs and is followed by a reward is more likely to occur again.* The principle reveals that with sufficient reinforcement a behavior becomes internalized and no longer depends upon external reward.

Since even inappropriate behaviors become internalized when reinforced long enough, it is important to identify and strongly reinforce behaviors that are desirable and directly incompatible, to replace the inappropriate ones.

The next section focuses on how to systematically incorporate these concepts into a structured program for use in your home, providing you with a powerful way to enhance your children's capacities for responsible behavior.

> *A child enters your home and for the next twenty years makes so much noise you can hardly stand it. The child departs, leaving the house so silent you think you are going mad.*
>
> ~John Andrew Holm

Chapter 4

Three Steps to Develop a Custom-Made Home Program

A program of constructive discipline is built on three steps, (1) specifying your expectations to your child, (2) making it good for your child to do as you expect, and (3) building your program into your family life.

Step 1: Specify Your Expectations to Your Child

In order for your child to learn to behave responsibly, your expectations must be very clear. If you sometimes say things differently from what you say other times, or if sometimes you insist on compliance and sometimes you don't, your children may really simply not understand. Or they may forget or confuse one set of rules with another. Remove all such confusion to assure consistent follow-through and compliance. Both require very clear statements about your expectations.

It is useful to separate your effort to establish your expectations for your child into two parts. First, carefully think about what changes you would like to achieve in your child's behavior. Second, write down exactly what you expect in terms that will assure compliance.

Identify Behaviors of Concern

To clarify your own expectations, start by considering what about your child's behavior concerns or bothers you. Parents report concerns about all sorts of behaviors; for example, children whining to get their way, fighting with siblings, leaving messes wherever they play, or failing to complete household chores or homework assignments.

Next, think about whether you have noticed any behaviors that don't seem to work well for your child or that may interfere with your child's own comfort or happiness. Since this means trying to see the world as the child does, this may require a bit more thought and even conscious observations over a few days to be sure you fully tune in to the child. Examples could include children with no friends because of bossiness or excessive shyness or children who seem to be angry and argumentative all of the time.

> *We worry about what a child will become tomorrow, yet we forget that he is someone today.*
>
> ~Stacia Tauscher

Also consider behavior that doesn't cause anyone else any obvious distress but which may interfere with your child's maturation in important areas. Examples could include children spending a lot of time on homework because of difficulty staying focused, children spending so much time watching television that they get no exercise, or children obsessively over-eating to the point of health problems. Also consider any other current challenges in your child's life that you might be able to help with, things such as learning to ride a bike or to dribble a soccer ball.

Finally, once you have thought through your own observations, consider whether your child may experience significant challenges that are unknown to you. Explain the program briefly and then ask your child for suggestions for other behaviors to include.

THREE STEPS TO DEVELOP A CUSTOM-MADE HOME PROGRAM

An eight-year-old girl who was asked by her parents to suggest challenges with which she wanted help wondered if the program could help her make friends. While her parents were astonished because they had always thought she had lots of friends, they recognized her serious wish and found a way to build an item focused on her concerns into the program. The girl did very well on the program, perhaps in part because her parents agreed to help her meet her own need for more friends.

A worksheet to help you with identifying behaviors to focus on in your program appears in Appendix 1, and the top portion appears here for easy reference during this discussion.

Identifying Target Behaviors

Child's name: *Johnny* Date: *July 9, 2011*

PORTIONS OF THE DAY	ISSUES IN CHILD'S BEHAVIOR
-- Before school --	
Getting up	*Have to call him 5 or 6 times to get him up*
Getting dressed	
Cleaning up (hair, teeth, etc.)	
Eating breakfast	
Getting off to school	*Never has his backpack ready so is always late*
Other (specify: *Distracted by TV*)	*Watches TV instead of dressing and eating*

Figure 2. Sample of Identifying Target Behaviors form - before school portion

The worksheet is organized by typical parts of the day. Under each, I have listed some of the associated tasks. The sample here displays the time before school, including items such as getting up and getting dressed because parents often identify problems related to these tasks. The space to the right allows you to write in details about your concerns for your child. In the sample you can see a few behaviors that other parents selected to help their child change.

Feel free to ignore or add tasks to best meet your own needs. For example, for the first task, "Getting up," if your child typically stays in bed until you've yelled half a dozen times and you finally have to resort to dynamite, or the child gets up but has pants but no shirt on, you might indicate that on the form. On the other hand, if your child handles the start of the day fine, just skip over that part and go on until you identify an area of some concern.

For each of your concerns, write a brief description next to the specific task, including when it occurs. For example, for "After school: coming home," one parent wrote, "Often misses bus." Another wrote, "Forgets his assignments at least twice a week." Include each behavior as many places as it applies. One parent wrote, "Teases Bridget," including it before and after school. Use more paper as needed to be sure you have covered all your concerns.

During later review, some parents report progress on some items but express dissatisfaction because what really bothered them wasn't on the list. To avoid this, the directions to the worksheet in the appendix urge you to be as thorough as you can be in identifying behaviors of concern. This is not to encourage you to suddenly become overly critical of your child. Rather, the idea here is to be sure that you identify all the possible candidates for items to include in your program so that you don't miss any. To that end, once you have completed going through the worksheet, there is a simple test (noted on the form as well) to determine whether you have thought of everything that you might want to include in your home program. Simply ask yourself this:

If we can help our child make all the changes we've written down, will there still be significant problems?

If in response you find something leaping to mind (for example, "Oliver pulls the cat's tail whenever he doesn't get his way") which doesn't fit the precise format of the worksheet, then find somewhere to add this new issue to the list – perhaps on the back of the page. Then ask yourself the test question again, repeating the cycle until you think of no more concerns. Reaching that point should not be construed as a promise that you will fix every concern you have identified, but rather as assurance that you now can focus your efforts to address those behaviors that matter most to you. When you find yourself saying "Hurrah" (that is, "if we could change everything on the list, then there would be no more problems"), you can feel confident you have completed the list well and that the next steps will be easier and more effective.

THREE STEPS TO DEVELOP A CUSTOM-MADE HOME PROGRAM

Define your Expectations for Your Child

Now that you have a complete list of behaviors of concern, the next step is to select the specific ones you will start working on. Simply go through your form item by item and select those that you consider to be most pressing or which you think will produce the most important benefits to your family.

> *Children are one third of our population and all of our future.*
>
> –Select Panel for the Promotion of Child Health, 1981

I should note that many behavioral specialists stress starting much more slowly, either focusing on only one item or perhaps on one behavior to increase and one to decrease. My experience questions this conservative notion for two reasons. First, because addressing so few items means that significant change may seem slow in coming, parents with numerous concerns about their children's behavior are likely to become discouraged and tempted to give up. Second, and more importantly, since most children and their parents seem to do fine by adhering to the following rule of thumb, there is no reason to risk such discouragement:

> *Plan on a maximum of one item per year of your child's age, with an upper limit of ten or so since more than ten tends to become unduly burdensome for most busy parents to manage.*

This means that for a five-year-old, five items is a good upper limit and busy parents of a twelve-year-old likely will find tracking ten or so items to be challenging enough.

Establish a Constructive Format

Producing lasting behavior changes in your children requires that they experience success, preferably from the very beginning. Once you are clear about which behaviors you will focus on, you are ready to move on to define exactly what you will consider successful behavior in each area.

The exact wording of your target behavior statements is very important, including sticking to this format:

> "____, *you are successful when* . . ."

This exact wording establishes the expectation that your child will succeed and focuses attention directly on what is required to make it happen. Even the word "when" makes it clear from the outset that you anticipate the success upon which further successes will be built.

But how do you write success statements to be sure that they are effective?

Write Well-worded Success Statements

There are three characteristics of well-worded, effective success statements:

1   Ensure that your expectations are realistically reachable

When defining your expectations, consider carefully what is realistic for your child, taking into account such factors as your child's age, abilities, and past successes. While this may seem obvious, in practice it isn't always so simple.

Suppose you are concerned that "Dwayne and Latisha fight all the time" and that in your home "all the time" means, on the average, hassles occur between them twenty times a day. To address your concerns, you could consider including this item in Dwayne's program:

> *Dwayne, you are successful when you don't fight with Latisha.*

However, when you think about your children, you realize that for Dwayne ever to reach that standard he would have to stop fighting with Latisha completely, an immediate change from 20 hassles a day to none. Since this does not seem at all realistic, you could rewrite your item to read:

> *Dwayne, you are successful when you don't fight with Latisha for an hour.*

Whether this will turn out to be realistic for Dwayne is uncertain, but clearly it is more likely he can avoid fighting for a hour than that he will never fight. Even if the two of them bicker several times during the day, Dwayne might be able to avoid fighting for an hour or two and he can start building up successes. Nonetheless, the expectation may have to be lowered even more for Dwayne to be able to succeed. For children who are used to fighting at least a couple of times each hour that they are together, the time frame may have to be reduced to just a few minutes for one success at the beginning.

The need to define expectations carefully can be discouraging for busy parents. Still, if you don't make the necessary effort to tailor your expectations to your

THREE STEPS TO DEVELOP A CUSTOM-MADE HOME PROGRAM

child's own capacity, chances are that you will continue to be dragged into the conflict many times a day. On the other hand, if you start small enough to assure that your child can be successful in this program, you can work toward longer and longer periods free of fighting.

Fortunately, parents' instincts tend to be very reliable with respect to their children. If you are realistic rather than wishful when you ask yourself how long your child can be expected to do a certain thing, chances are you'll be pretty close with your answer. Thus, when you first decide on a time frame, ask yourself if you can imagine your children going without fighting for that long. If your reaction is "no way," then adjust your expectations downward until you can say, "Yes, Dwayne probably can do that."

You have probably recognized that keeping track of frequent successes can be very demanding to manage. Fortunately, there are ways to reduce the burden with a simple timing device.

> *Imagine that you are busily working on your taxes while your two kids play across the room. In your program, they are each successful for every half hour they play together nicely. You begin work knowing that any hassles will catch your attention but worrying about remembering to reinforce the kids each time they have done okay for a half-hour. As you get deeper into the paperwork, you suddenly realize that you'd forgotten the kids and the stress of trying to keep track of two important things at once builds up. Still, gradually the demands of the forms consume your attention entirely. A half-hour and then 40 minutes come and go and you don't notice. Finally at 45 minutes the children begin to complain loudly about each other's unfair play. You perk up and a glance at the clock tells you that you have failed your part in the program.*
>
> *What do you do now? The children had succeeded at 30 minutes but if you reward them while they are bickering, you reinforce their misbehavior. Recognizing your failure, you likely feel guilty, an awful feeling that you may set about avoiding by focusing on the children's failings with comments to yourself like, "Darn it, those children are old enough to be able to get along. It's their fault we have to mess around with this dumb program, after all!" With your guilt converted to anger, you may lash out and likely will consider dropping the whole program.*

Fortunately, with some planning a simple kitchen timer or an inexpensive wristwatch with a built-in timer can be set to alert you when the established time has elapsed. You set it, get on with your business, and respond only to misbehavior or when the timer alerts you.

In this example, when the timer goes off at 30 minutes, you go to the children, praise their good play together, comment on the credits they have earned, reset the timer, and go back to what you were doing. Both in this example and in general, the whole interchange after the timer rings is likely to take no more than a minute or so, freeing you to engage fully in other activities.

The general point here is to find ways to minimize unnecessary intrusions from the program and its demands. While this may seem to be a little thing, I have seen it make the difference between parents giving up and parents continuing a very effective program.

This illustration points to another very useful rule of thumb:

> *Set the goals for your child* ***as high as you can*** *(that is, don't greatly under-challenge children), but* ***as low as you must*** *in order for the child to be successful* ***no less than about a third of the time.***

While this is a useful standard, in practice if you underestimate your child and success comes easily most of the time, you may find you are so pleased with the results that you won't mind that you are providing more reinforcement than might have been required. On the other hand, if you set the standards too high, things won't go so well but you can take comfort in knowing that there will be plenty of opportunities to refine your expectations to assure success.

> *What's a good investment? Go home from work early and spend the afternoon throwing a ball around with your son.*
>
> ~Ben Stein

Time factors. Most items in your program should include a defined time frame for success in order to assure there is no confusion about your expectations. An item lacking clarity regarding time might be:

> *Emma, you are successful when you have your homework done on time.*

The vagueness in this statement would allow Emma to work on her assignment until midnight or even to leave for school with the intention of finishing it between classes. While this might be acceptable for some parents, probably most parents would be quite uneasy with either alternative, and they would be tempted to fuss at Emma to get her work done, risking, in the process, giving her attention for procrastination.

In order to avoid this, specifying an exact time is important. An improved statement for this example might be:

Emma, you are successful when you have your homework completed for all your classes by 8:00 p.m.

Note that this modification includes an important element: the item does not define the time when Emma should start her work, but rather specifies a deadline for completion. There are two reasons for stressing this distinction:

First, alternatives to specifying a deadline for completing a behavior are either to leave it up to the child (read that as "never") or to state when the behavior should start. Anyone who has told a reluctant child to "get started on your homework" is likely to have had the experience of sending the child to bed hours later with the homework still undone. This approach invites stalling and procrastination in children inclined to push the limits. One reason for this is that it sets up a power struggle between parent and child, and typically children can "win" such struggles since it is relatively easy to "start" and still not actually to do much of anything.

Second, knowing when something must be done allows the child to plan how to manage time and parental expectations. Consider this item:

Joshua, you are successful when you have the entire lawn mowed by noon on Saturday.

This item makes it clear that if Joshua would like to meet friends Saturday morning and still be successful, he can do so by planning ahead. If it is acceptable to his parents, he might elect to mow Friday afternoon, easily meeting the deadline and freeing him for other activities. Thus, the deadline allows him an appropriate level of control over his own life, within boundaries clearly specified by his parents, providing a key experience for learning responsible behavior.

You will likely recognize that as important as specifying deadlines for successful completion of items is, adding a time factor can also add extra work for you in monitoring your child's behavior. Fortunately, some advanced thought and planning, taking into account your child's age and abilities, can minimize this extra effort.

For older children, those capable of telling time, the timing process itself is typically fairly easy. It is a matter of clearly specifying the time frame for success and then noting whether the child has met the standards on time. The item for Joshua above is an example. For some other items keeping track requires a bit more effort, for example of how many times during the day Dwayne doesn't fight with his sister. In this case, the parent should make a note of each success as it occurs to assure none is forgotten, part of the home program we are working towards.

For younger children, who can't tell time by a clock, it is important to choose a realistically short time frame and then to use a timing device that will help the child keep track. A simple kitchen timer, for example, will serve this purpose. A suitable sample item might be:

> *Samantha, you are successful when you have all your toys put away from the family room by the time the timer rings.*

Show the child the timer the first time you use it and let the child see it run for the specified length of time to provide a sense of how long you have allowed before applying it to a behavior. Then reset it for the task at hand. Many young children see beating the clock as a game and their successes provide an opportunity for rewarding them with both praise and credits, such as a token.

> *There's nothing that can help you understand your beliefs more than trying to explain them to an inquisitive child.*
>
> ~Frank A. Clark

With such young children, watch for several potential complications.

When setting the criteria for success, it is important to consider how long you think a task would typically take for your child and then set the time limit a bit longer than that – but not a lot longer. For instance, if your four-year-old girl is to pick up her toys from the family area and if you think it would take her five or six minutes to do it if she stuck to it, you might set the standard at eight minutes. If you are more generous, say setting it at 20 minutes, the child will be likely to lose track of the task long before that and thus be less, rather than more, likely to succeed. Allowing a little extra time, on the other hand, might well increase the likelihood of success within quite appropriate limits.

THREE STEPS TO DEVELOP A CUSTOM-MADE HOME PROGRAM

At first, little ones are likely to ignore the timer and you may be tempted to "remind" your child, maybe even repeatedly. While this is pretty natural, it provides the child attention for failing to do the task and keeps the responsibility on the parent, rather than teaching it to the child.

Some children quickly learn that they can reset the timer and avoid performing on time. To avoid this fudging, use a tamper-proof timer if you have one. If you don't have such a device, explain that the timer is to help the child keep track but that you are using a clock or watch for the same purpose. Show the child how the two timers work the same. The first time or two, you will need to be sure that you actually watch the clock or, even better, that you set a separate timer of your own. The timer on a kitchen range or on some wristwatches will work just fine. The idea here is to make it clear from the outset that the clock is an objective monitor so the child's energy goes into completing the task, not into trying to manipulate you.

All this is to assure that your expectations are defined so as to be realistically reachable by your child and so that the conditions support meeting them, the first of three characteristics of well-worded success statements.

2   Ensure that your goal statements are worded positively

I have already discussed the importance of focusing on behaviors that you do want, including those selected because they are incompatible with behaviors that you don't want. This idea is so important that it warrants restatement as one of the prime characteristics of well-written success statements.

Since it is so natural to focus on the unacceptable behavior that you wish to eliminate, it is very easy to allow negatives to slip into your statements of expectation.

An earlier example considered the item:

Dwayne, you are successful when you don't fight with Latisha.

That wording seemed to demand perfection and therefore was asking too much. To make the statement more realistic, the item was amended to read:

Dwayne, you are successful when you don't fight with Latisha for an hour.

While this change does respond to the need to be realistically reachable, it focuses attention entirely on what Dwayne is **not** to do while completely failing to define the desired behavior. Fortunately, it is pretty simple to fix this with a statement that is both realistically reachable and positive, such as:

Dwayne, you are successful when you **get along with** *Latisha for an hour.*

Because giving attention to a behavior that you wish to eliminate works against your intended goal, it is important to follow this example to define what you do want your child to do. Think about the failure of the teacher to stop the little boy from pulling the hair of a classmate and the success achieved once the focus changed to making it good for him to sit at his desk. As in that situation, a positive focus sets the stage for your child to succeed.

3   Ensure that the criteria of success are very clear

Write your statements of expectations so that both you and your child will know exactly what is expected. Achieving this will make it clear to your child that there is nothing to be gained from haggling with you about whether or not your expectations have been met, freeing the child to focus on the task itself.

> *Each day when a mother told her son to take the trash out, he would respond, "in a minute, Mom." When a few minutes later she would tell him more sharply to "take the trash out," he would reply, "But Mom, I'm in the middle of my favorite TV program." Still later she would yell at him but take no action, a pattern that would continue for a couple of hours. You might ask, "Why would either of them waste two precious hours to avoid a few minutes of work?"*
>
> *The likely answer: it appears that after the first few minutes of each interchange, the issue evolved from the trash to a power struggle over who was in control. Sadly, nobody could win in this situation. Even when the mother gave up and her son didn't have to take the trash out, he felt bad about the conflict with his mother, and he had wasted time that he could have spent with friends. On the other hand, even when the boy finally gave in and took the trash out, the mother was left still frustrated and feeling like a poor mother, and she also had wasted a lot of time.*

A home program with clear focus on the mother's exact expectations could have avoided this unhappy interaction and fostered a warm and cooperative family environment.

The necessary elements for clearly stated items include **who, what, how much, by when, and how you will measure success.** (I might note that the same elements are included in many constructive human interactions, such as when skilled managers give assignments to members of their staffs.)

Including these elements assures focus and energy on the successful behaviors, in the process eliminating bickering and badgering about whether the child was successful. Here is an example of an item with clear criteria:

> *Alejandro, you are successful when you have the trash out of every room in the house by 5:00 p.m. on Tuesdays.*
>
> | *Who?* | *Alejandro . . .* |
> | *What?* | *. . . have the trash out . . .* |
> | *How much?* | *. . . from every room in the house . . .* |
> | *By when?* | *. . . by five o'clock on Tuesdays.* |
> | *Measure of success:* | *Checking the trash cans and the clock.* |

In order for this – and pretty much any other approach to parenting – to succeed, it is essential that you mean exactly what you say. Thus, if the criteria include being done "by 5:00 p.m." and your child gets done at 5:10, I urge you not to accept that the task has been successfully completed. This is based on the certainty that if ten minutes late is okay today, the next time it is likely to be 20 minutes, and then 30, and so on. No matter how easy-going you are, there is likely to come the time when the delays lead to frustration and an argument. At that point your child may, ever so innocently, ask, "Why the big deal?" since being late had been okay before. And the child would have a point: how can the child know what you really expect if your expectations are fluid? Avoid teaching your child that it pays to fudge, badger, or negotiate, by meaning what you say – this time and every time – and by acting accordingly.

Deal with Potential Complications

When you cannot meet all three characteristics

Unfortunately, it is not always possible to fulfill all three criteria of realistically reachable, positive, and clearly-stated standards of behavior. To illustrate, consider our previous example which began with:

> *Dwayne, you are successful when you don't fight with Latisha.*

Since it is unrealistic to expect Dwayne to go from 20 hassles with his sister every day to none, we modified the expectation to read:

Dwayne, you are successful when you don't fight with Latisha for an hour.

While more realistic, this focused attention on fighting, the very behavior the parents wish to eliminate. To fix that flaw we modified the statement to read:

*Dwayne, you are successful when you **get along with** Latisha for an hour.*

With this change we defined for Dwayne realistic expectations for more positive interactions with Latisha.

But here is the rub: twelve reasonable people could have a dozen different notions about what it means to "get along with" his sister. Unfortunately, nearly any effort to define that phrase tightly is likely to rely on such notions as "don't hit," "don't tease," or "don't argue," all negatives. I have challenged hundreds of parents in my classes to come up with a better way to tightly define such an item and have yet to hear a good alternative.

We must conclude that we cannot always accomplish our goal of writing realistically reachable, positive, and perfectly clear goal statements. Considering that fact, use this hierarchy of standards to guide your efforts:

- It is *critical* that your expectations be *realistically reachable*,
- It is *extremely important* that your expectations be *worded positively*, and
- It is *very important* that the criteria of success be very *clearly stated*.

Avoid haggling with your child

Solid as these guidelines are, they leave a potential weakness in our system. Success statements that lack clarity tend to invite haggling and complaints, distracting parent and child from the underlying goal, for example:

I did too get along with her, but she was making faces and slid over to my side of the car so I just pushed her back on her side.

Since such complaints tend to draw focus to arguing and away from the program, **never respond to or participate in haggling with your children**.

Because, as attractive as this sounds, is easier to say than to accomplish, some clear guidelines are needed to help you stay out of such interactions. To avoid

THREE STEPS TO DEVELOP A CUSTOM-MADE HOME PROGRAM

being sucked into haggling by children pushing the limits, be clear in your own mind about these concepts:

First, since you are more experienced than your children are, it is appropriate for you to fairly determine whether your expectations have been fulfilled.

> *Each day of our lives we make deposits in the memory banks of our children.*
>
> ~Charles R. Swindoll

Second, your judgments do not have to be perfect. If you avoid at any costs being what your children would consider "unfair," your children will learn that with clever enough arguments you will give in. You may be especially vulnerable if you can't put into convincing words exactly why you are saying "no." You can be sure that far more children have suffered from parents' unwillingness to make and stick to a firm decision than from being denied some special privilege, however dramatically they might complain at the time.

Third, respect your child's need to understand by explaining how you made your decision, and keep clear in your mind that making a decision and sticking to it does not mean you are cavalier about your child's feelings.

Fourth, if your child challenges your decision and you think you can explain more effectively, do so, simply and clearly.

Fifth, if your child continues to complain or haggle with you, follow this very effective guideline:

> *Do not explain yourself to your child more than twice unless you have a very clear reason to think that after the next explanation your child will understand and accept your decision.*

Anytime you continue to respond to your child's fussing after a second explanation it is highly likely that you have moved from providing *information* to offering *justification* to your child. Has your fussing child ever responded to one of your repeated "explanations" by saying, *"Gee, Mom, now that you explain it like that I see why I shouldn't be able to stay up until 2:00 a.m. Golly you are smart."*? If you accept that you must justify yourself to your child, you have put your child firmly in control by agreeing that your decision counts *only* if you can convince your child that you are correct.

Sixth, whenever your child continues to fuss and complain after you have explained sufficiently, convey this important message:

*Well, Christopher, I've explained the best I know how and I am sorry if you don't understand, but **that's just the way it is**.*

While there may be many ways to say the same thing, this wording is actually very effective and makes it clear to the child that there is no more room for discussion. Take special care to to avoid what may seem like very similar statements, such as "Because I said so" or "Because I'm the parent, that's why." Both statements focus on you rather than on the decision, directly challenging your child to battle for power, the opposite of your goal.

To make sure the distinction is very clear, read the statement I have suggested aloud, then compare it aloud to "Because I said so" and "Because I'm the parent, that's why" and notice how different they sound – and even how different you feel when saying them. I recommend that you stick close to the wording shown above, at least early in your experience with this approach.

Assure a constructive interaction

Once you have conveyed this message, avoid further discussion. If your child continues to fuss, as many will, there are several ways you can terminate the interaction:

1   Leave the room yourself.

Some children will follow parents anywhere they go to keep the argument going but for others leaving the room can be quite effective in ending a heated interchange between parent and child.

2   Remove the child from where you are.

Sending or taking a child to an area away from you can also be effective if this can be managed constructively.

But what if your child continues to argue with you and circumstance make it impractical for you to either move away from your child or move the child away from you?

3   "Tune out" the child until the fussing stops.

THREE STEPS TO DEVELOP A CUSTOM-MADE HOME PROGRAM

Stop for a moment as you read this and notice all that is going on in your immediate environment. What do you hear? What do you smell? What does it feel like to sit as you are? How much had you noticed these things before? To pay attention to your reading, you had to ignore everything except this page, e.g., television sights and sounds, barking dogs, honking horns, and fussing children.

Your capacity to tune out fussing and other annoying behaviors provides the basis for a simple but effective technique to disengage when your child continues to argue or whine after you have explained your decision. The technique provides a means of carefully controlling your response to the child even in the face of persistent fussing.

To get a feel for how it can work, imagine transforming yourself into a robot, with all your own characteristics but without feeling annoyed about your child's inappropriate behavior. Without that emotion, there would be no reason to react to your child's fussing. As a robot, you would be free to go about whatever you have to do without interacting with the child.

> *Conscience is less an inner voice than the memory of a mother's glance.*
>
> ~Robert Brault

To be effective, "tuning out" your child must be done calmly and continued long enough for the child to recognize that there is nothing to gain by persisting and that it is better just to go on to more interesting things. If the fussing continues and finally you react, your reaction will reinforce the persistence, and you can expect your child to fuss even longer the next time.

> *A woman with two very young children and a baby reported that her children seemed constantly to be clamoring at her knees, particularly while she hurried to prepare dinner. She felt she could not remove the children from her nor could she leave them in the kitchen. Taught that she could tune out the fussing, she reported she was able to withhold her reaction and soon her children drifted off to other activities, freeing her to complete her work. As a bonus, she found her efficiency in the kitchen increased enough to give her more time to attend directly to the children.*

Some children will react to being tuned out rather sharply and may even insist their parents don't love them. It is important not to get pulled into such comments because doing so will prolong the confrontation with no positive outcome. Tuning out, when done calmly and impassively, is not about rejecting your child, but rather is a means to convey by your actions – which indeed do speak louder than words – that the interaction is over, far more loving than participating in a never-ending argument with your child.

One additional note: children, particularly very young ones, watch faces to see how others are reacting, even running completely around a parent turning away from them. You can use that observation to enhance the effect of tuning out your child by simply turning your face away. If circumstances prevent you from doing that, at least keep your face blank – or robot-like.

It is also important to reinforce the desired behavior, the second component of our overall strategy. A few minutes after things have calmed down, go to your child and reestablish contact. However tempted you may be to do so, this is not a time to lecture about cooperation or to otherwise comment on the previous interaction. Rather it is a time to show the child that your love and concern remain strong even though you did not give in to the haggling. The contact at this point should be warm and should demonstrate that the previous hassles are over. A brief comment about something the child is doing, a pat on the head, or any other simple and warm gesture will be enough.

The goal of all this is to teach your child to focus on successfully completing the assigned task rather than on attempts to manipulate you. In the process it also teaches the child how good it can feel to complete tasks responsibly while at the same time reducing the fear of being too much in control of adults.

One word of caution: **do not attempt to use this approach unless you are confident that you will be able to persist** and stick with your decision to withhold responding to the child. If the child succeeds in wearing you down and can keep the haggling going, the lesson learned is likely to be: *If a little fussing is not enough, then more might work.* Over time such interactions will lead to major family conflict.

To summarize, well-constructed target behaviors use the format " , *you are successful when. . .*" and include *realistically reachable expectations which are put in positive terms with the criteria of success clearly defined.*

THREE STEPS TO DEVELOP A CUSTOM-MADE HOME PROGRAM

Sample Target Behavior Lists

To clarify this discussion, target behavior items suitable for the home program of a nine-year-old boy appear in the box below.

Johnny Jones - nine years old

Johnny, you are successful when:	Credits
1. you are up, dressed, and done with breakfast by 7:30	10
2. you are home from the bus by 2:45	10
3. your school chart shows by your teacher's initials that:	
a. you cooperated during reading period	5
b. you were friendly with kids on the playground during recess	5
c. you turned in your math on time, at least 75% correct	20
4. you stay friendly with Billy (for each 30-minute interval)	5
5. you have the trash out of every room in the house by 5:30 (Mondays, Wednesdays, and Fridays)	5
6. you stay at the table and eat your dinner within 20 minutes	15
7. you are in bed and quiet: by 8:30	10
by 9:00	5

Figure 3.   *Sample set of target behaviors for a child of reading age*

There are several things to point out about the list:

1. The list includes seven items for this nine-year-old boy consistent with the rule of thumb of no more than one item per year of age. In practice, you may not choose to regiment your child's day this thoroughly, unless the child's behavior is very troubling. This number of items is included in this example simply to illustrate the wide variety of target behaviors that might be included.

2. Item 3 consists of three parts, all related to school. This can be considered one item for counting purposes since the parents still only have one item

to keep track of. All items are reflected on the school card (discussed in detail below), which folds right into the rest of the program.

3   Since Item 4 specifies that staying friendly with Billy will be counted in 30-minute intervals, the exact number of successes possible will vary from day to day. Some days the children may be together very little while on other days, especially weekends, they may be together for many hours and so could earn lots more credits. That will be important to consider in determining the number of credits to be traded for specific rewards, discussed below.

4   Item 5 indicates that Johnny is assigned to take the trash out only three days a week, illustrating how easily the program can be tailored to address a family's specific requirements.

5   Item 7 further illustrates the program's flexibility. Johnny's parents prefer him to be in bed at 8:30, but sometimes he really wants to stay up until 9:00 to complete a TV program. The parents recognize that they can increase their son's interest in the home program by allowing him a choice of staying up a bit later or of earning more points by going to bed earlier. Of course if they really wanted him in bed at 8:30 each night, they would not include this variation, but they have observed that he has been responsible and seems to do fine the next day after staying up a bit later.

While generally the same in overall structure, target behaviors for children younger than reading age tend to look somewhat different. To highlight some differences, I have included a sample listing for a five-year-old girl in the box.

There are a several specific aspects of this younger child's list to consider:

1   This list includes five items, as many as can be expected to work well for a five-year-old child. As with Johnny's list, this one contains more items than a typical family might choose to include but they are all shown to illustrate the variety of items that could be included.

2   One obvious difference in this listing is that the child earns "tokens" instead of "credits," which provides the child a more concrete indication of success than numbers on a chart, not very meaningful to one so young.

THREE STEPS TO DEVELOP A CUSTOM-MADE HOME PROGRAM

Sally Smith - five years old	
Sally, you are successful when:	Tokens
1. you are completely dressed by the time the timer rings (15 minutes)	1
2. you play quietly in the family room while the baby sleeps (per 30-minute interval)	1
3. you stay at the table and eat all the food from your plate by the time the timer rings (20 minutes) – per meal	1
4. you have all your toys put away in the family room by the time the timer rings (10 minutes)	1
5. you stay friendly with Billy (for each 30-minute interval)	2

Figure 4. Sample set of target behaviors for a pre-reading age child

3 Another difference is evident in that only one or two tokens are offered since younger children tend not to comprehend bigger numbers.

4 Item 3 indicates, in parentheses, that Sally can earn a token for each meal. As with Johnny's school items, this behavior is counted as only one item even though it likely occurs at least three times during the day. This can be done because it is not particularly more challenging to the child and it does not add much to the parents' tasks of monitoring the program.

5 Item 5 represents a departure from all the other illustrations in that it does not, in itself, identify a specific behavior. This item further illustrates how the program can be tweaked to meet specific family's needs. In this case, it actually amounts to a kind of bonus – or miscellaneous – category that might be included by parents with a young child whose undesirable behaviors show up in enough different circumstances to make it difficult to define success behaviors ahead of time. It allows each parent to specify on the spot an instance in which the child can succeed by cheerfully doing what is assigned to her.

It must be stressed that such an item places considerable demand on the parents. Each time they give the child a special assignment they must *clearly* and ahead of time present *realistic expectations* in *positive terms*, all the while also maintaining their usual monitoring. As a result, such an addition to a program should be used sparingly.

Because establishing clear expectations for children can sometimes become more complicated, in the next chapter you will find responses to several questions about the process posed by parents with whom I worked.

Step 2: Help Your Child Want to Do What You Expect

Your next challenge is to make it good – provide reinforcement – for your child to comply with your expectations. Theoretically, you could follow your child around all day and reinforce every success as it occurs. In practice, since you cannot be with your child all the time, this isn't possible. Nor would it be good for your child if you could, since an important aspect of maturation is learning to tolerate and accept delayed gratification.

But if you don't reward your children instantly, how can you take advantage of the vital power of reinforcement? What you do is essentially the same thing that happens in the adult world: for each unit of work an adult completes, he or she earns a portion of a paycheck, and for each item on the target behavior list your child completes, you provide a defined number of "credits." For example, when Brittany has her room suitably cleaned by noon on Saturdays, she earns 10 credits. Over the course of the day, she can earn as many credits as are included on her target behavior list.

But why would your child want to work for credits? Here also the answer parallels what happens in the adult world: just as an adult can trade portions of a paycheck for goods and services, your child can trade credits for some object or privilege of interest. Your challenge, then, is to establish a system that will allow your child to receive suitable reinforcement, even when you are not at hand all the time.

Assign Credit Values for Each Target Behavior

To develop an effective system, your first task is to go item-by-item through your target behavior list to determine how important each item is so that you can assign a suitable credit value to each. It is important to consider this task both from your own adult perspective and from your child's perspective.

Your Perspective

For every parent, there are likely to be items on the target behavior list that are of considerable importance, and there might be others that are of interest but not as compelling.

THREE STEPS TO DEVELOP A CUSTOM-MADE HOME PROGRAM

For instance, for a family living in a high crime area, an item such as *"Aaron, you are successful when you are in the house within five minutes of being dropped off at the bus stop"* may be considered critical for the parents. For the same family an item such as *"Aaron, you are successful when you have all your toys picked up from the family room by 8:00 p.m."* may be desirable but not nearly so critical.

Your Child's Perspective

Similarly, for every child there are some tasks that might seem very burdensome and there likely are others that might be an inconvenience but not a big deal. For example, even though an item such as *"Nicolas, you are successful when you clean the backyard of all dog waste by noon on Saturday"* may take only a few minutes to complete, Nicolas may really hate doing it. On the other hand, while it might take much time and effort to complete an item such as *"Nicolas, you are successful when you have the entire back yard mowed by noon on Saturday,"* the boy may actually enjoy doing it so it would require fewer credits to nudge Nicolas into action.

Once you have determined which items matter most and which items make the biggest demands on your child, weigh all such factors and assign credits to each task, using your best sense of the level of reinforcement required for your child to succeed on each item as well as for the program as a whole.

Age Differences

Assign credits according to your child's skill levels, which generally will be related to age and other maturational aspects.

For the older group

For children who are able to read and to understand numbers a bit, generally those above six or seven, work toward assigning about 100 points to cover all the tasks expected on a typical day. There is nothing magical about this number, but older children seem to strive more for larger numbers of credits. The number 100 is easy to work with while larger numbers can become cumbersome and smaller ones may not have as much impact. Use your decisions about the relative importance of each item and assign credits accordingly, with numbers ranging perhaps from five points for the easiest and/or least critical items to 20 or more for those that are more difficult and/or you consider most vital.

Once you have assigned credits to each item, add them up to see what a typical day could total. If it comes out at 85 or 120, for instance, there is no reason to worry about it; the 100 is just a rough starting point. The total you have for your program simply provides a basis for determining how many credits you will require the child to trade later for material rewards.

> *If we would listen to our kids, we'd discover that they are largely self-explanatory.*
>
> ~Robert Brault

As you work this out, though, be aware that you may not be able to determine the exact number of credits your child can achieve on a given day because of variations in when the items apply. For instance, an item stressing children getting along with each other for half an hour could be counted a few times on a week day and many more on a weekend. None of this will cause a big problem since the exact number of credits your child can earn does not matter a lot. You just need an overall sense of how many credits can be achieved and therefore what level of rewards you will need to provide.

For the younger group

For children who can't yet read and understand numbers, those below six or so, assign one token for most behaviors and two tokens only for especially important behaviors. Most children beyond three or so, generally the lower limit for a formal program, will understand that two is more than one and any two-credits item will catch the child's attention and provide extra incentive.

Since the concept of "credits" won't mean much to younger children, use something more concrete, a token of some sort. Plastic poker chips, buttons, small pieces of colored paper, or stickers are all possibilities. For young children, avoid small objects that they might be able to swallow. Generally coins are not a very good idea. Also make sure that your child does not have unearned access to whatever you use. Arrange for some sort of a suitable "bank" for your child's tokens, such as a sturdy envelop or small can.

Note that even for younger children it is important to keep a written record of successes to guide your effort as you progress through the program. Further, the record will assure that you provide all of the rewards that are earned even if your child misplaces the tokens.

Three Steps to Develop a Custom-Made Home Program

Provide Meaningful Reward Choices

Once you have assigned a credit value for each item, your next task is to develop a catalog or list of rewards. While this concept is straightforward, there are several important aspects for you to consider:

Consider What Your Child Cares About

The most important step is to be sure that your child is interested in the reward choices offered. We parents might all agree that a trip to an ice cream store for a sundae would be a great choice. Nonetheless, if the specific child has no taste for ice cream, then it won't matter what parents think. To assure the choices you include in your list will have the needed impact, tell your child about the plan and ask for input. For example:

> *Hermione, we want our family work better. We are going to make it easier for you to cooperate and so that we all can enjoy each other more. We have a new program that lists what we expect you to do, as well as when and how to do each task. This program is to help you do these things on your own. Each time you complete one of the tasks successfully, you will earn a certain number of credits (or tokens). When you have earned enough credits, you can trade them in for something special.*
>
> *We have worked out the list of things you are to do and how many credits you can earn for each task. Now we want to make sure you are interested in the reward choices. Rewards could be toys or books or special activities or maybe you can think of other things. What would you like us **to consider** putting on a list of rewards that you can choose from?*

The phrase "to consider" is emphasized so that both you and your child understand that *you* will decide what ends up on the list. Your child is free to suggest any reward at all, but you will decide whether or not to include it.

Consider What You Can Provide

If any of your own ideas or those of your child cost money, consider whether you can comfortably afford to provide them if your child chooses them.

> *A father described his son as "out of control." Eager to change things, the parents agreed that the boy could choose renting a motor boat to fish*

59

with his dad. The boy did well, earned this reward, and the two went off to the lake where the father discovered that renting a boat was more expensive than he'd expected and more than he thought it was worth. When he suggested they fish from shore and use the savings later for a deep-sea fishing trip, his son agreed and they fished from the bank.

The following Monday morning the father called to berate the program we set up for them, reminding me that it "was supposed to make things better, not worse." Later in the office he said that the fishing trip had ended unremarkably, but the next day his son became sassy and testy. By that evening he seemed to the father much as he had seemed before we began, and Monday morning the boy had refused to go to school.

In private the boy described how disappointing it was to sit on the bank watching other boys steering boats around the lake, and he felt that his dad had broken the agreement of the program.

The moral: be realistic about what you include on the reward list, no matter how generous you are or how much you want your child to improve. If your child earns a reward that you can't afford or one that you will resent providing, you can expect the child to feel cheated. This would be much the same as you might feel on payday if your employer told you the company couldn't afford to pay you. Be reassured that this program does not require parents to be wealthy. I have worked with people who had no money for extras like toys but who still had very effective programs. So, choose rewards that fit your family finances with the full confidence that you will make the program work using your choices.

Consider Your Time Limitations

In addition to assuring you can afford any money involved in rewards, agree to reward choices only if you are confident that you'll have time to provide them. Even things from a store have to be purchased and if you are too busy to arrange shopping within the time limits defined in your reward list, your child will feel cheated. Not only is a child who feels cheated unlikely to be fun to live with, but also you will have undermined the effectiveness of a program that, handled properly, offers powerful support for your efforts to develop a responsible child.

THREE STEPS TO DEVELOP A CUSTOM-MADE HOME PROGRAM

Consider Your Family Values

Along with resource limitations, consider whether a requested reward fits your value system. Sometimes parents are so concerned about correcting their child's difficult behavior that they may agree to things that they really don't want for their child.

> *At their 12-year-old son's request, worried parents added a raunchy R-rated movie to his reward list, since "all my friends got to see." When he had earned enough credits for the movie his behavior was better and his parents were no longer desperate and could see things more clearly. They were left with a dilemma, wanting to honor their agreement but unwilling to allow their son to see the movie. Fortunately, negotiations during a family therapy session led to an agreement. The parents, in effect, bought out the boy's contract with a number of pretty grand substitute rewards.*

The moral of this story: think ahead and don't violate your own values.

Consider Constraints on Delivering Rewards

Some rewards may not be so easy to deliver exactly when the child reaches enough credits to deserve them. To avoid disappointing your child, include a time frame or other limit in the description of the reward choice.

> *Naomi has elected to trade her earned credits for a trip to Sea World and she supposes the family will leave for the park the moment she earns enough credits – even at 8:00 o'clock on a school night.*

With such an expectation, waiting until morning might seem really unfair, and waiting to the weekend, or even waiting for weeks, might result in feeling downright cheated. To avoid this, include appropriate limitations for the item in your reward list. For example:

> *A trip to Sea World within a month of achieving xxx credits.*

A child unable to tolerate this clearly-stated delay would never choose it, far better than having the child choose it expecting immediate fun and ending up frustrated and upset by having to wait.

Consider the Value of Special Time Together

Among the most potent rewards you can offer your child is special time with family, especially parents. Over my years of working with troubled children and families, I frequently have dealt with children who seemed so angry with their parents that they would hardly speak to them. To the parents' immense surprise, many of these children ended up working hard in their home programs and then choosing rewards that involved time with parents. Whether or not you happen to fit that description, I hope you'll consider adding at least a few reward choices involving special time with family. Some simple sample rewards:

> *A half-hour playing catch with Mom*
> *15 minutes with Dad, reading a book selected by Josephine*
> *A family cookout at the park*

Parents who follow through despite any misgivings frequently find that their children choose such rewards, even if they previously had typically avoided family activities. There may be two reasons for this:

> The program tends to change the emotional climate in the home so that warmer feelings come easier.

> Spending time with parents appears to feel significantly different for a child who has earned the choice to do so.

Whether either of these conjectures fits your family, the worst that can happen if you include such reward choices is that your child will not select one, not a problem since having the choice is what matters.

Consider How to Keep Your Child Interested

It is important that your child always finds something on the list that is enticing. To assure success in this aspect, follow this rule of thumb:

> *To assure that your child always has something of interest to work toward, include at least five choices on your reward list, ranging from some simple items requiring only a few credits to some grander ones requiring a larger number of credits.*

The wisdom of this guideline is evident in this example:

> *It is September and a ten-year-old boy who loves baseball is saving his credits for a baseball glove. Before he reaches his goal, the World*

THREE STEPS TO DEVELOP A CUSTOM-MADE HOME PROGRAM

Series is over, and suddenly his interest shifts from baseball to football. If this boy's reward list were limited to the glove, he might well lose interest in the program. However, with several other enticing reward choices on his list, perhaps some related to fall sports, he can shift his focus and continue his progress toward becoming a responsible child.

Among the five or more choices of rewards, include items that can be attained with a day or so of modest successes. Other items should provide incentive for sustained effort. Choices for younger children should include some that can be selected fairly soon after the responsible behavior occurs. But even children as old as 12 or 13 can be so dubious about the reward system that they need to trade in their credits daily for a time before they can trust the system and work longer for a bigger reward. What matters is not how grand the reward or how long the child works for it, but rather that the child stays interested and continues to complete the expected behaviors. Remember that every time the behavior occurs and is reinforced, it is more likely to happen again and is on its way to becoming an internalized behavior.

Consider Differences for Younger Children

Children from three or so years of age to six or seven will understand the connection between their behavior and the reward only if the reward comes soon after the behavior occurs. That means that they will need evidence of benefits for their efforts almost immediately while older children soon learn the association between behavior and reward, and hours or even days can pass between their acts and the associated rewards.

Since you will need to reward younger children more frequently, it can be a challenge to come up with enough meaningful choices. One flexible choice with considerable staying power is a simple and inexpensive grab bag. Select several small toys, party favors, or other objects and place one item in each of several small paper bags stored together in a larger bag or basket. When your child elects to trade tokens for a grab bag, the reward consists first of choosing a bag, then the surprise, and finally the toy to use at will.

SAMPLE SETS OF REINFORCEMENT LISTS

The box below displays a sample reward list for reading-age Johnny Jones and shows typical examples of what some parents have included in their lists. The list illustrates the basic requirements: a set of several items ranging from simple to grand and the cost in credits to earn each.

Johnny Jones - nine years old

Johnny, you can trade your credits for: Credits	Credits
1. your choice of dessert for dinner (within three days)	100
2. 50 cents (40 cents to spend and 10 cents to save)	200
3. a trip to the beach (on the weekend)	350
4. a family outing to get ice cream (within a week)	500
5. one night overnight at a friend's house (within two weeks)	1000
6. a new baseball glove	1500
7. a fishing trip to the lake with Dad (within a month)	2000
8. a new snorkel and fins	3000

Figure 5. Sample reward list for a child of reading age

Note that several items include clauses that define further what Johnny can expect should he elect to trade credits for a certain item. For example, Item 7 alerts both him and his parents that the fishing trip can happen any time within a month – though the father would be well advised to plan ahead and deliver sooner if he can. Your own reward list will likely look quite different but should still include the elements reflected in this sample.

The following box displays a reward list for a younger child, this one for a five-year-old girl. Basically, this list is the same as Johnny's except that the items fit a little girl, and it refers to tokens instead of credits. Parents, of course, must fit the content to the specific interests of the child. Later, I will discuss a simple way to help a young child understand how the "cost" for each reward relates to the amount of tokens earned.

In order to address potential complications in establishing appropriate rewards for children, I have included a number of questions posed by parents and my responses in the next chapter, after discussion of the third step.

THREE STEPS TO DEVELOP A CUSTOM-MADE HOME PROGRAM

Sally Smith - nine years old

Sally, you can trade your tokens for: Tokens	Tokens
1. one stick of sugar-free gum 5	5
2. an ice cream cone 10	10
3. 15-minute game of your choice with Mom or Dad 15	15
4. a grab bag toy 20	20
5. going out for ice cream (within a week) 25	25
6. a special toy approved by Mom and Dad 50	50

Figure 6. Sample reward list for a pre-reading age child

STEP 3: BUILD YOUR PROGRAM INTO YOUR FAMILY LIFE

Your next task is to establish how the program will operate in your family. Done poorly, the program can demand much family time and attention. Done well, it can be minimally intrusive and can contribute to a warm atmosphere with special time together each day. There are two parts of making the program work smoothly, the behavior chart and the daily review.

DESIGN YOUR BEHAVIOR CHART

Operating your program on a daily basis requires a workable system for monitoring your progress. A simple but carefully designed behavior chart provides the needed tool and serves several important functions:

First, the chart provides a ready reference for each of you, detailing your expectations for your child. To assure it is readily available throughout the day, post the chart in a prominent place in your home where your child can check it as often as necessary to carry out the assigned behaviors.

Second, the chart allows an easy way to display, in a place you all will be used to looking, any changes required to keep you on track toward your goals.

Third, the chart records the child's performance and credits earned on each item each day and includes a line for totals, clearly displaying your child's progress toward meeting your goals.

Fourth, the chart tracks the child's progress toward rewards. This tracking heightens the child's anticipation of pending rewards (reinforcing in its own right) and alerts the parents to prepare to provide the rewards as they are earned, avoiding unnecessary and disappointing delays.

Fifth, the chart provides you with a permanent record of your program, including all modifications you make and when you make them You will use this record frequently over time to monitor your progress, as is discussed in detail in Chapter 8 below. Some parents talk about how interesting it is to look over the charts even years later to revisit their efforts and their child's progress. Make a point of storing your charts by date for each reference later.

The chart can be a simple grid with space for each of the needed elements. A sample blank chart appears in Appendix 2 as a model, and two illustrative versions appear below. Reviewing the column and row headings will clarify the structure. What matters with the chart is not how fancy it is, but rather how clearly it lays out your program and how convenient it is for you to use.

A sample chart for our mythical nine-year-old Johnny appears below.

Some of the boxes are shaded (though corner-to-corner X's would work as well) to designate times when an item doesn't apply. For instance, shading for Item 7 on days other than Monday, Wednesday, and Friday shows that Johnny is expected to take the trash out only on those three days and avoids any chance of confusion between non-counting days and days when he didn't succeed. Success on Items 5 and 6 is measured in 30-minute intervals, and small hash marks could be entered for each success as it occurs, in each day's box, to track how many times Johnny stayed friendly or played outside. Then the hash marks would be counted and converted to the number of credits earned for the day.

> *If you want children to keep their feet on the ground, put some responsibility on their shoulders.*
>
> ~Abigail Van Buren

THREE STEPS TO DEVELOP A CUSTOM-MADE HOME PROGRAM

Home Behavior Program

Johnny, you are successful when: for the week of _October 18_ 20 _09_.

Target behavior	Cred	Mon	Tue	Wed	Thu	Fri	Sat	Sun
1. you are up, dressed, and done with breakfast by 7:30	10	10	10	10	X	10		
2. you are home from the bus by 2:45	10	10	10	X	10	10		
3. your school chart shows by your teacher's initials that:								
a. you cooperated during reading period	5	5	X	X	5	5		
b. you were friendly with kids on the playground during recess	5	5	X	5	X	5		
c. you turned in your math on time, at least 75% correct	20	X	X	20	20	20		
4. you stay friendly with Billy (for each 30-minute interval)	5	″ 10	″ 10	‴ 15	″ 10	‷ 20	‶‶‶ 35	‷‷ 30
5. you have the trash out of every room in the house by 5:30 (Mon, Wed, and Fri)	5	X		5		5		
6. you stay at the table and eat your dinner within 20 minutes	15	15	X	15	X	X	15	15
7. you are is in bed and quiet: by 8:30 by 9:00	10 5	5	10	X	5	5	10	X
Daily total		60	40	70	45	80	60	45
Credits used					500 *			
Running balance		410	470	510	580	125	205	265	310

* Used 500 credits for a family outing for ice cream

Figure 7. Sample set of target behaviors for a child of reading age

Charts for younger children look very similar to those for older children except for the number of items and the number of tokens. A sample for a five-year-old girl is presented below, for convenience as you read about the next step.

67

HOW TO RAISE DISCIPLINED AND HAPPY CHILDREN

Home Behavior Program

___Sally___, you are successful when: for the week of _July 12_ 20_11_

Target behavior	Cred	Mon	Tue.	Wed	Thu	Fri	Sat	Sun
1. you are completely dressed by the time the timer rings (15 minutes)	1	1	X	1	1	1	X	1
2. you play quietly in the family room while the baby sleeps (for each 30 minutes)	1	2	2	3	2	3	1	3
3. you stay at the table and eat all the food from your plate by the time the timer rings (20 minutes per meal)	1	2	1	1	2	2	2	3
4. you have all your toys put away in the family room by the time the timer rings (10 minutes)	1	X	1	1	X	X	1	
5. you stay friendly with Billy (per 30-minute interval)	2	2	X	4	2		6	8
Daily total		7	4	10	7	6	10	15
Credits used			15*				50#	
Running balance	52	59	48	58	65	71	31	46

* Used 15 tokens to play a game with Dad   # Used 50 tokens for a stuffed animal

Figure 8.   Sample behavior chart for a pre-reading age child

IMPLEMENT YOUR DAILY REVIEW

With your behavior chart at hand, your next step is to establish and maintain a daily review to tie all the elements of the program together. The review typically takes less than five minutes for one child and less than ten for two or three children.

First, set up a regular time each day for the review. The time of day that the review occurs doesn't matter much. What does matter is that it happens every day at a time when all members of the family can attend. If your schedule truly

THREE STEPS TO DEVELOP A CUSTOM-MADE HOME PROGRAM

makes this impossible, establish the best schedule you can but be aware that you may have to make extra effort to assure the full benefit of this procedure.

> *When you have brought up kids, there are memories you store directly in your tear ducts.*
>
> ~Robert Brault

Second, if you have a parenting partner, both of you should attend each day's review and alternate which of you takes the lead in order to take full advantage of your joint strengths. This practice will also serve you well on those occasions when you simply can't both be there since the one there will be able to carry out the review the children expect. If you have no parenting partner, you can still have a fully powerful program although clearly you will have more responsibility, something you don't need me to tell you.

Third, at the time you have selected, gather the family together and use the chart to guide you systematically through reviewing the success of each item that applies for that day.

A Sample Scenario

To get you started, here is how to make your daily review work.

First, for each item on your target behavior list determine whether the child was successful by reading the item aloud. For example:

> *Was Johnny up, dressed, and done with breakfast by 7:30 this morning?*

Each question is answered by whomever knows, perhaps the parent who just read the question. The question is not directed to the child and to avoid tempting your child to fudge or to try to negotiate, accept any answer your child offers only if you can verify it independently. Once the answer is clear, if Johnny was successful, comment on the success. For example:

> *Oh, yes, I remember. You got done so fast you had time to watch some cartoons. You seemed so happy this morning that it made my day get started really well, too. And look, Johnny, we've just started, and already you have earned ten credits. Way to go!*

This simple comment effectively ties together for the child the expected behavior, your social reinforcement, and the credits that stand for the material reinforcement, all the elements of a successful program.

Second, if another parenting figure is there, that person can add praise and further comment on the credits. For example:

> *Wow, Johnny, good work! I wish I could have been here. My day got off to a kind of bum start. And boy, if you keep it up, you'll have enough credits to get that new baseball glove in no time at all.*

The second parent's comments add social reinforcement to the benefits from the first, while reference to the reward Johnny is working toward ties in the material reinforcement as well.

Third, be prepared for times when your child does not successfully complete the task as assigned. As before, whoever knows answers the beginning question aloud briefly; generally a simple "no" is enough. The parent with the chart writes an "x" on the chart in the correct spot, and then just goes on to the next item. This won't come naturally to a lot of parents since we all seem to have some great lectures saved up for situations such as this:

> *Gee, Johnny, if only you would get started on time and try a little harder and were more like your cousin and wouldn't goof off so much and showed a little initiative and cared about your family and didn't play so many of those stupid video games, then maybe you'd do something right once in your life and wouldn't be on your way to a living in abject poverty and misery like your Uncle Herman – because you forgot to take the trash out on time...*

I trust this harangue is exaggerated enough to suggest my view of this approach. It is an oddity of the human condition that when we praise, it tends to be short and to the point while our criticisms tend to go on and on and on.

The idea is that an unsuccessful child should experience your brief but unenthusiastic response. If you have a flair for the dramatic, leave a brief pause so that the difference between praise and no reaction can sink in, but stifle the urge to point out the difference since doing so again provides attention for failing. In contrast, make sure that for successes, your child feels your strong, warm reaction and is aware of the credits earned. Remember, for your program to work, you have to make it more rewarding for your child to do what you expect than to do the opposite.

THREE STEPS TO DEVELOP A CUSTOM-MADE HOME PROGRAM

Continue through your list in this same fashion, praising successes and mentioning but not dwelling on the rest of the items.

Fourth, once you have gone over each item on the child's list of behaviors, add up the credits for the day. When you first start the program, comment on what the child can do with the number of credits earned. For example:

> *Great, Johnny, you already have 80 credits. Another good day like this and you could choose dessert the next night, or you could save your credits a couple more days and choose 25 cents.*

The goal of this comment is to help your child fully grasp the association between earned credits and choices from your reward list. Within a few days, your child may well be more up on this than you are, and you may need only to comment on progress toward the reward known to be of interest. Since your child's preferred reward may change for a variety of reasons, from time to time check on the current interest. For example:

> *Johnny, you have 320 credits. Are you still working toward the mitt you've been talking about, or do you have something else in mind now?*

If the child continues to show enthusiasm for the baseball glove, you can talk about what fun it will be when he has earned it. If the child expresses interest in some other reward, then you can show enthusiasm about it and maybe even reinforce the advantages of having choices:

> *So, Johnny, you decided you'd rather work toward a trip to the park to play catch. That will be fun. Isn't it great that you have so many choices and that all your good work can pay off in so many different ways?*

Consider Your Child's Age

All of the notions discussed so far apply in a straightforward fashion to children from ages six or so up to early adolescence. That middle group can read and thus can follow the chart, but they still require a good deal of parental guidance and support. For both the younger and older groups, there are special considerations not true for the middle group.

For the younger group

Several developmental factors must be accommodated for children up to age six or so. Since a younger child cannot read the chart, cannot remember all the details, and cannot tell time to meet deadlines, parents must provide timely instructions. However, frequent reminders can blend into nagging and an attempt to motivate the child, directly competing with the program's incentives. Further, nagging gives attention and can provides a sense of control, allowing the child to meet those important needs by *failing* to take responsibility. Remember that a child who does only what is demanded by repeated parental urging is not taking personal responsibility for anything.

Younger children can't link rewards with their earned tokens. They typically do understand simple board games and this can be used to help them. On a piece of paper draw a trail of circles or squares connected by arrows. Then draw or paste a suitable magazine picture for each of your child's reward choices beside the trail, at the number of tokens required to earn the reward. Your child will quickly learn to place one earned token on each space to determine progress toward each reward. Appendix 3 provides a sample game board, though yours does not need to be quite that fancy.

For the older group

As children reach early teen years, consider their advancing capacities to assume more responsibility even when they seem rather irresponsible. Progress in this area is particularly important for children facing ever increasing challenges in their dealings with the world beyond your home. Even middle-school children already face many weighty but often unrecognized responsibilities, including how to relate to members of the opposite sex, how to respond to offers of drugs and alcohol, and how to plan for their futures. Their home programs, then, should provide them increasing levels of responsibility and correspondingly wider ranges of privilege.

To support maturation in your older children, focus as much as possible on broader areas of responsibility even early in your program and increasingly over time. For example, for a child who does not show much capacity for independently managing responsibilities, you may need to define the several tasks associated with cleaning up the kitchen after dinner. On the other hand, for a child showing more maturation in this area, simply assigning the child the task of cleaning up the kitchen after dinner would foster more independence than enumerating each small task required to finish the job.

On the reward side, define areas of privilege for children demonstrating the capacity for larger areas of responsibility. For example, a trustworthy teen might earn a reward of getting home an hour after school ends if there are safe and wholesome activities available and other circumstances are fitting.

THREE STEPS TO DEVELOP A CUSTOM-MADE HOME PROGRAM

As your child progresses to take more responsibility, consider developing a written contract, a modification of the basic program chart discussed earlier. When you think you and your child are ready, meet for open negotiation of a contract, discussing the reasons to accept or decline each idea. While you retain control over the final agreement, allowing children increasing levels of say in their own lives will support your goal of preparing your child for full adulthood. Once you have completed the contract, have your child sign what amounts to a pledge to complete the designated tasks, an action most adolescents take very seriously. Then it is your turn to sign, taking your signature equally seriously. An example of a contract is presented below.

Agreement between Kelly and Mom and Dad
Effective: May 23rd through July 23rd, 2011

I, Kelly, agree to the following:	We, Mom and Dad, agree to the following:
1. I will attend all of my classes on time every day (or arrange with my parents for an official excuse if I must miss any).	1. We will allow Kelly to spend time with friends after school until 5:00 p.m. (unless we need her home earlier and then we will provide her all the advance notice possible).
2. I will clean the kitchen to family standards every night by 7:00 (unless I get permission ahead of time to have someone else fill in for me).	2. Kelly may decide when and how she cleans her own room but she is responsible to assure that no food, drink, or dirty dishes accumulate there.
3. I will introduce my parents to any friends I ask to go out with and will provide them with the names and telephone numbers of my friends and their parents.	3. We know it is important for Kelly to spend time with friends and we will give careful consideration to her requests to go out with them.
Signed: _____ Date: _____ Kelly	Signed: _____ Date: _____ Mom Signed: _____ Date: _____ Dad

By July 23rd we will review progress and either extend this agreement or revise it to best meet all our needs.

Figure 9. Sample behavioral contract between a 15-year-old teenager and her parents

Some Additional Considerations

It is best to record failures with an "x" rather than a "0" to avoid tempting children to fudge a higher score, such as could happen by simply adding a "1" in front of the "0," as I have seen on a few charts.

Some children make negative comments during the review of another child's chart. Sibling rivalry often reflects the belief that parents don't have enough love to go around. A child who believes that will struggle to monopolize whatever amount there is, and in the process to undermine any siblings who are seeking the same love. With this in mind, whenever you see rivalry in your children, you can make it clear that each child is loved and valued. Your home program provides a concrete way for each child to succeed and thereby achieve social reinforcement without detracting from another's successes.

In addition, while doing your daily reviews with two or more children at the same time, you can also deal with a child's negative comments, in a manner that could increase more supportive sibling relationships. When one child says something non-supportive, disregard the negative content and respond only to the child's attention and interest. For example, you might say:

> *Felix, I'm glad you are interested in how well Rachel is doing. I hope she will want to hear how you are doing, too, when we get to your chart.*

Most children will at least calm in the face of such a comment. As you go along, continue to reinforce any comments or interest consistent with sibling cooperation and avoid negative reactions to less warm comments.

If these efforts are ineffective in reducing negative comments between siblings, at least for a time meet with each child separately, thereby avoiding hurtful comments that could diminish the impact of your praise for successes. As your program takes fuller effect, you are likely to see the rivalry diminish and you can try again to hold your reviews jointly.

Since circumstances in specific homes can make implementing a home program more challenging, I have included discussion of a variety of questions raised by parents related to building the program into family life in the next section.

Chapter 5

Challenges in Developing a Home Program

While I have attempted to be clear in describing the steps to building an effective home program, I know that some of the concepts and ideas may still seem rather vague and that their full richness may not yet be evident. To flesh them out better, what follows are discussions of some questions from parents about each of the three steps involved in developing a custom-made program for your family. Each question is presented here with just enough alterations to assure privacy for those involved.

Step 1: Challenges in Specifying Expectations

Our 11-year-old daughter has a very messy room and when we check it, she says it's clean but we think it is still too messy. What can we do about that?

Parents tend to see this kind of disagreement as about their standards for their homes and family, while children see it as about their rights and freedoms. When you build your home program, your main challenge is to tightly define what you mean by a "clean room." Since your daughter typically fails to meet your standards, make sure that each item is realistically reachable, considering both her abilities and her history of actually doing such tasks. If she never does the job as you expect, then you may need to break it into parts and provide reinforcement for each part. For example, you could divide "clean your room" into "hang up your clothes," "put away your toys," and "vacuum the floor." Define each item to include a suitable deadline and specify how you will judge her success. These smaller tasks are much more likely to be completed but will require that you monitor the progress more closely to assure you provide praise and credits for each completed task.

When you have completed refining your items, it should be clear whether the room is clean or not clean by checking its appearance. Since your daughter may attempt to continue the haggling, be prepared to simply inform her of your judgment about her successes and then disengage to end the haggling.

Our program is working pretty well but it still bugs me that I can't talk on the phone without Susie (7) acting up. Any ideas about how to handle this?

Typically children who demand attention during phone calls have learned that they can get mom to react in those situations. Some may resent the attention mom gives to the other person. Whatever the cause, the approach to dealing with it is pretty standard. Start by defining a success behavior, for example:

> *Susie, you are successful when you stay quiet and calm for X minutes while Mom is on the phone.*

Once the item is added to your program, provide Susie her credits for each X minutes that she succeeds. Set a timer to alert you to when X minutes have passed and if your phone call runs longer than X minutes, excuse yourself briefly, go to Susie, praise her, and provide her with earned credits, or at least tell her they will be put on the chart. While this may be inconvenient in the beginning, it will be better than constantly being interrupted and over time it will teach Susie to tolerate longer periods while you are on the phone.

One other point: if your conversation ends in less than X minutes, I suggest that if Susie knows you were on the phone and it was for more than a minute, you consider her successful. That way Susie won't feel cheated that the conversation stopped before she could succeed when trying to remain quiet, and she will also have more successes to build on.

Our two sons, seven-year-old Austin and nine-year-old Hunter, constantly pick at each other. It's hard to figure out how to write an item that will stop it. We doubt the program can help with something that has been going on for years. Any ideas?

CHALLENGES IN DEVELOPING A HOME PROGRAM

Many parents report concerns about children bickering. Initially I had misgivings about how to deal with this in a positive way. It is hard to avoid focus on all the things children should not do but it turns out that many parents find success in this area. The item may be as simple as:

Hunter, you are successful when you get along with Austin for X minutes.

Include a similar item in Austin's chart, taking care to define a realistically reasonable number of minutes for each child. Then monitor success and provide the specified praise and credits for each success.

A parent's love is whole no matter how many times divided.

-Robert Brault

Since "gets along with" is somewhat vague, why do so many parents report success with this sort of item? Careful consideration reveals three ways for children to succeed and only one way for them to fail on this item:

- If Hunter really wants to succeed, even if Austin doesn't care about his credits, the bickering will likely fizzle; it really does take two to tangle.
- Similarly, if Austin wants to succeed, even if Hunter doesn't care, any fussing will likely stop because Austin won't participate.
- And, of course, if both want to succeed, things will go fine.
- Therefore, only if both boys happen at the same time to have no concern about earning their credits will bickering between them continue. Three out of four represents pretty good odds.

Even children who fight all the time typically like being together and separating them often provides extra incentive for them to calm themselves. If you make it clear that being together is a privilege achieved only through behaving appropriately toward each other, you may find that your children change their behavior, though maybe only after testing the limits a few times.

If the bickering between Austin and Hunter goes beyond what is acceptable to you, tell them that since they are unable to behave appropriately, you are going to help them by putting each in a quiet area where he can calm down before returning to other activities. Separate the children enough that they can't keep the hassles going by taunting each other, even from a distance.

We have an eleven-year-old (Lin) and a six-year-old (Mi Li). Lin is always picking on Mi Li. Then Lin gets upset when we punish her and says Mi Li is pestering her all the time. How can we deal with this problem?

Much of what I said in the previous answer applies here, though the sizable age difference may make it likely that at least some times Lin actually does not want to be around Mi Li. A girl her age needs time with age-mates, away from her younger sister who has such different interests and skills.

Be sure you have included age-appropriate and realistically reachable target behaviors in each girl's chart to deal with the problem. Once that is done, take time to observe carefully what really goes on between the girls. When an older child picks on a younger one, often the younger has learned to retaliate against the older until getting a reaction. When the older child reacts negatively, the younger screams and that brings parental help. Sometimes when the parents' backs are turned, the younger child snickers to the older one, enraging the older child, who feels victimized by the younger child. That rage, in turn, makes the older child all the more resentful and more sensitive to even a little pestering. This sort of vicious cycle can take over family life with the parents increasingly annoyed at the older child, whose distress and need for positive attention grows and grows.

If there is any chance of such a pattern in your home, you will need to make changes to stop the cycle. One big part of that is to be sure each child is clear about what positive behaviors will win your attention and praise. The other part is to remove the children from each other if they continue bickering after you have told them to stop – without your blaming one or the other. It also is important to model for the children your own calm manner.

Our seven-year-old daughter, Melinda, is very shy and has no self-esteem, especially at school. How can we help her feel better about herself?

You have raised concerns about both shyness and self-esteem. Sometimes these two are linked, but not always, so I will discuss them separately.

Generally self-esteem is directly connected to an individual's own experience of her capacity to deal effectively with the world around her. Because of that, the more successes Melinda has, the better she will feel about herself. Your home program provides a very straightforward way for you to define age-appropriate responsibilities. When Melinda is successful, you can then provide honest praise and material benefits for her successes as evidence to her of her abilities.

CHALLENGES IN DEVELOPING A HOME PROGRAM

With reasonable success, over time – perhaps not all that much time – Melinda is likely to begin seeing herself in a new, more positive light. Central to this is for her to see you basing your praise on real behaviors, not just on your wish to be supportive, which she might discount because "parents have to say that."

For some children who appear shy, seeing themselves succeed will increase their confidence, and they will interact more capably, and therefore they may no longer seem so shy.

At the same time, some shy children seem to be happy and to get along fine. Observe Melinda carefully over a period of time to see if shyness itself is causing her any unhappiness. Some parents who were themselves shy suppose their children are as sad as they remember being, and they may work hard to solve a problem that may not be a big deal for their children. In fact, the parents' extra effort could backfire because focus on shyness could convince the child there really is something wrong. Thus, while shyness can be a very big burden for some children, some children seem to be shy by nature. Even with help to be more comfortable with others, some may never become outgoing. Watching and listening to how the child feels, both during interactions with peers and while alone, may be a help in deciding how much attention to give to this issue – though it can be difficult to be sure even after careful observation.

Fortunately, one of the strengths of the home program approach is that you don't have to know with certainty how distressed Melinda is about being shy. By carefully designing your program to start where your child is, you can encourage her without burdening her with extra worries. Because the program amounts to an invitation to achieve whatever you define as success behaviors, Melinda can progress at her own pace, and she may come to attempt new interactions with others, free of undue pressure or pushing.

You can encourage Melinda to interact more with other children by defining exactly what you hope for her to do. Take care to assure that what you are asking is realistically reachable, basing each step on your observations of Melinda's past behavior. An example of a first-step target behavior item for a child who appears to have few or no peer interactions might be:

> *Samantha Jane, you are successful when you learn the name of one of your classmates.*

For a child who seems to know her classmates and the neighbor children but seems to spend all her time alone, an item might be something like:

Destiny, you are successful when you play with Monica for 15 minutes the next time she and her mother come to visit.

Later on, or maybe sooner for a child who seems to be ready, this sort of item may be appropriate:

Briana, you are successful when you invite one of the neighbor children over to play.

Start with your first item where Melinda is and add a small challenge to encourage going a bit beyond what is usual for her. Base your choices on what you have seen her do and on your sense about what she appears capable of doing even when she seems reluctant.

Several times here I used the word "encourage" because these programs are structured to give each child a choice of whether to complete each task. Unlike some approaches, we do not hassle a child for failing to complete a task. Rather, we attempt to make it good for the child to succeed. In the case of a shy child learning that it can be okay to interact with others, we can carefully define the expectations, based on what seems realistic. The child, then, can elect to comply and earn your praise and credits toward a tangible reward or not to comply and simply earn no praise or credits. Because of this, you need not be so concerned that you may be pushing your child beyond her limits. Of course if she never completes the item as defined, you will need to reconsider the level of expectation, lowering it to be more realistic or, perhaps, upping the number of credits that Melinda can earn for succeeding.

If after all of this you remain concerned, I'd suggest you discuss the situation with your child's physician or with a mental health professional. This step can help you determine whether your daughter will benefit from some sort of counseling intervention or whether she may simply be temperamentally reserved in her interpersonal interactions.

My 11-year-old son, Jorge, moves as slowly as he can whenever we tell him to hurry up. We tell him over and over that he causes us to be late and also how much better his life would be if he'd move faster so that he has time to do other things he likes, but we aren't getting anywhere. Ideas?

You have described an almost classic example of a child controlling his parents by dawdling. Jorge gets lots of attention and may get a sense of control by causing you to repeat "over and over" how he inconveniences you. While your reaction surely is understandable, it almost certainly is self-defeating because it reinforces the very behaviors you dislike.

CHALLENGES IN DEVELOPING A HOME PROGRAM

The remedy is in the basics of the home program. Define success behaviors to address your concerns, including deadlines for each part. Your description suggests that you will have to start by accepting a fairly low level of progress for each item. As an example, you might consider an item as simple as:

Jorge, you are successful when you have your school backpack ready for next day's school by your 8:00 o'clock bedtime.

And then you can focus on some of the steps necessary for him to be ready to leave on time in the morning, such as:

Jorge, you are successful when you are up and dressed by 7:00 a.m.

Once you have your list completed, be sure to reinforce successes each time they occur and also be sure to withhold reaction to his stalling behaviors. Once your program helps your son complete even one part of his morning routine, you can build on that to a second part, and so on. I hope you will find that some progress, however small, is more encouraging than it is to stay in a pattern that is likely otherwise to go on and on or even get worse.

> *Anyone who thinks the art of conversation is dead ought to tell a child to go to bed.*
>
> ~Robert Gallagher

While you are working to replace your current style of frequently telling Jorge to hurry, with a program of reward for meeting your deadlines, you are likely to have days when you must leave the house before he has gotten himself ready. For this interim period, anticipate when this problem is likely to occur and allow time to intervene briskly to finish getting him ready. On a day when it is clear he cannot succeed, go to him and without any comment (turning yourself on "robot"), complete the necessary tasks for him. For instance, if he is not fully dressed, put him into the remaining clothes, then hustle him on to the next step and finally out the door. He is likely to protest, perhaps even loudly, and you must be prepared to remain calm and focused on simply moving things along. The point here is to assure your son is ready when you need him to be while avoiding meeting any of his needs for attention or control.

Because of the potential problems that can occur if your son achieves too much control over adults, I suggest you reread the discussion of control issues in Chapter 3.

Ravi is getting the trash out on time now, but we are getting tired of always having to remind him that the deadline is almost there. How can we get him to do it on his own?

While it is understandable that you want to assist your son, if Ravi is able to read and tell time, he has the basic skills to fulfill his own responsibilities. However, by reminding him prior to the deadline for completing the task, you are not allowing him the opportunity to succeed – or fail – on his own.

I suggest that you change your tactics. Start by telling Ravi that you are no longer going to remind him and that he is responsible to get the trash out on his own and on time. Since he has had your reminders as a crutch in the past, he may not succeed the first time on his own. If that happens, go to him very soon after the deadline has passed and tell him that since he missed the deadline, he no longer has a choice about when to do it. Then instruct him to "take the trash out now." If he protests, help him to his feet and guide him through the process, providing as much supervision as necessary to get the trash out. Be careful in the process to interact as little as possible so as to avoid giving unnecessary attention to Ravi. This approach will make it clear that it is a responsibility he must fulfill and therefore it is in his best interests to do it correctly and by the deadline so that he can earn his credits.

We get so tired of eleven-year-old Thomas telling us every day how unfair we are for making him do so many chores since none of his friends have to do any. What can we do to stop this?

Lots of children complain about how mean their parents are for giving them chores their friends don't have to do. Perhaps it is the friends who are mistreated if they really have no chores. First, they are not getting the chance to contribute to their family's well being, and second, they are not learning to see themselves as responsible people. Both of those omissions leave big holes in a child's preparation for taking a place in our society. My guess is that most parents, when they think about it, will agree with that sentiment.

So, how can you deal with a child who has a different idea of what you should expect of him and who is all too ready to say so? The start of a constructive response is to accept the child's feelings, which you might express like this:

Thomas, I understand you don't like the idea of having to do chores. . .

CHALLENGES IN DEVELOPING A HOME PROGRAM

Of course accepting the feeling is not the same as agreeing that your child should not have to do any chores and that you are an ogre for expecting him to. It is a good idea to say so by continuing the above remark:

> *. . . but in our family each of us has responsibilities and we work together to get things done. We know you are able to do your part for our family and it is our job to help you get used to doing it. Because we understand that it is kind of hard for you to get yourself started on your chores, we have made our home program to help you. You will earn credits for finishing chores as assigned and you can trade them for rewards.*

It will also be useful to acknowledge the rest of the complaint so that Thomas doesn't suppose you missed his powerful logic, perhaps adding this:

> *We are sorry if your friends' parents don't feel they should teach your friends to help their families. We think it is important for you to learn such responsibilities, just as we did when we were growing up. We will continue to teach you the things we think are important so you will grow up to be the responsible person we know you can be.*

After that, avoid further objections so that you don't risk reinforcing complaining and stalling. You really don't have to listen to complaints after you have dealt with them. If the complaints continue, you could remove your child from the family area to give him time to regain his control.

Our children, four-year-old Celia and seven-year-old Malcolm, are very picky about what they eat, so I end up preparing different things for each of them. How can the program help me out of this bind?

Getting children to eat what the rest of the family eats is a common problem and may contribute to the alarming increases in childhood obesity. In my experience, it is not terribly difficult to modify eating habits in children up to age 11 or 12. After that age, many have convinced themselves that some foods are awful even if they've never tasted them. Fortunately, your children are young and your home program can help you deal with your concerns.

While your goal is to teach your children to eat what the rest of you eat, I suggest that you broaden your focus to helping them fit into your family's whole mealtime routine. Plan to include in your program standards based on how your family handles mealtimes and work to reinforce each child for meeting those standards. For example, while some people may talk about the "dinner hour," probably very few actually devote that much time to meals.

You should set your own time limits according to how long you typically spend at the table – unless you happen to eat so rapidly that little children won't be able to match you.

First define exactly what you expect of your children. Based on experience with lots of families, here is a prototype target behavior item that covers several very important elements related to cooperating at mealtime:

> *Malcolm, you are successful when you stay at the table and calmly eat all the food on your plate within X minutes (or, for four-year-old Celia . . . by the time the timer rings).*

To help you tailor your own statements to your family's style, I will discuss each element separately.

Expecting a child to *"stay at the table"* will be no challenge to one who already does so. Still, since it is important to the overall effort, I encourage you to include the phrase in your definition of success; at worst it will simply be four extra words and at best it will avoid your child's testing you in a new area. If your child typically leaves the table and wanders back later to eat some more, I urge you to tell the child ahead of time exactly how things will work before you start using this item in the program. The message should very clearly state that in your family you stay at the table during meals, and that when you leave the table, the meal is over for you. I'll come to the implications of that in a moment.

"Eating all the food on the plate" may be easy for some children, while many others, including your children, regularly complain about what they are served. Even if you were willing to continue cooking separate meals, it seems utterly unfair to you. Further, it cannot be in your child's best interest to be so picky, demanding, and controlling since that style will be impossible to maintain at school or in other interactions away from home.

To change your children's expectations, start by stressing to each child the new way things will work in your family. Next, carefully plan the first meals you will serve using the program. To assure that it is realistic to expect your children to eat the food on their plates, combine a small amount of the favorite food for each with small amounts of foods you want to serve but that have led to resistance in the past.

For example, suppose Malcolm likes only macaroni and cheese and hates vegetables, fruit, milk, and other nutritious foods. For the first few meals on the program, put a modest amount of macaroni and cheese on his plate, along with no more than two or three green beans and a slice of apple, and serve them with just a little glass of milk. The idea here is not only to make the first step relatively easy but also to assure that he cannot satisfy his hunger by eating only his favored food. Tell him that he can have more of what he likes when he finishes what is on his plate, so that he need not go hungry.

> *The important thing is not so much that every child should be taught, as that every child should be given the wish to learn.*
>
> ~John Lubbock

Considering the extent of eating problems in our society, our expectation that Malcolm *"eats all the food on his plate"* requires further comment. Our goal is to teach children to participate more naturally in family meals and, in the process, to attend to their own bodies' needs by eating just the right amounts of nutritious foods. To achieve that goal with your children, you must avoid associating mealtime and eating with power struggles or supporting the belief that the children can only tolerate junk foods. Take care not to press your children to eat too much – or too little – to meet their health needs. To assure you are helping your children to a lifetime free of struggle about food, maintain a matter-of-fact focus on eating to live and not on power struggles.

The third aspect of the target behavior is to assure the meal is eaten *"within X minutes."* Teach each child what you expect by setting the timer or pointing out on the clock how long each has to finish eating. Remind them that they must stay at the table for the entire meal and that leaving means that child's meal is over. Also remind them that success means a clean plate within the time limit and that, when done, they may have more of anything you served. This does not mean either child can demand any other type of food. The family should eat as you typically do, stifling any urge to prod your children to hurry so that you don't reinforce dawdling.

If you plan to have dessert, serve your children a share if they stay at the table and complete the meal you served with enough time for sweets within the time limit. This way of handling dessert makes it like the rest of the meal; anything other than the original food on the children' plates is available only if the first serving is completed. Avoid making dessert a direct reward for eating, a connection which may play a role in some childhood obesity.

Another point: to provide your children with the best chance of success, all family members should stay at the table and eat all the food on their plates, and each should fill his or her plate accordingly. The one exception for most families would be the cook, who may have occasions during meals to jump up to get things. This special role should be explained in simple terms to the children, with focus on how the cook benefits everyone by those efforts.

So far so good. Whenever either child eats the food provided within the time limit, your job will be to provide reinforcement for the success by praising and by commenting on the credits or tokens earned for being successful. Avoid lectures about how the child should have learned this long ago. You can amplify the reward value by commenting to others at the table about how pleasant it is to have your child there and eating so well. And if the child requests more of food he or she likes, the extra food itself becomes an additional reward.

This is the basic outline. At following meals, use the same idea, but gradually add a bit more of the foods you would like each child to eat. Over a matter of a few days, broaden the range of things you add, eventually serving what the rest of the family eats. Depending on each child, this could take a good while. Be patient and do not push too fast. Once a child gets used to eating what is presented in a reasonable time, you may notice that the choice of specific foods seems less and less important.

But what do you do if one or the other child complains or leaves the table? The answer is already mostly defined for you: the meal for that child is over. Once the child is gone, remove the plate from the table and meet any complaints by calmly repeating that once the child left the table the meal was over. Likely the child will look greatly pained and complain of being hungry – maybe even "starving" – and you can respectfully repeat that food will be available at the next meal of the day. You are likely to hear a good deal of fussing and it is very important that you do not participate. Start by telling (not asking) the child to leave the room. If there is resistance and continued complaining, calmly remove the child from the room and return to the table as soon as you can.

You may find yourself feeling very mean at this point and feeling sure that your child will suffer from hunger. You may be tempted to provide some snacks along the way to the next meal. If you do that, you will have become an "enabler" of the very behavior that you set out to eliminate, that of picky eating. While it may seem mean to withhold food, there are very few children in our part of the world who will suffer any real harm if they miss whatever part of a meal they don't eat in this situation. Parents may need to make exceptions for children with diabetes or acid reflux or other eating related problems. For their parents, a discussion of the problem with the child's physician is in order. While pickiness about food for such children can be serious enough to complicate their health care, solving this problem is all the more important for them. Almost any other child will survive if they don't eat a whole meal. Far better a day or two with a little hunger than ongoing battles about eating, potentially the seeds for all sorts of long-term difficulties.

Typically parents who follow these steps in a calm and non-punitive fashion find that their children rapidly learn that it is in their best interests to eat as their parents expect. Success leads to improved nutrition and family interactions. It also helps prepare children for eating with people who may not serve macaroni and cheese for every meal. With these experiences, children gain confidence for meeting the social world on equal terms.

Step 2: Challenges in Establishing a Reward System

For most families, arranging the reward side of a home program is pretty straightforward. Still, there are a number of concerns that can arise that aren't so obvious. To assure you have support in thinking through any complications in your own family, I have included a number of examples of questions raised by other families, all focused primarily on the reward side.

We developed a program and started it, but our ten-year-old Abby just isn't interested enough in any rewards to make it work. What can we do?

Generally each of us is willing to complete a task if the reward meets a need that is important enough. People even go to war and put themselves in harm's way to protect what they hold dear. Therefore the challenge is in determining what those things are that Abby values most.

> *Imagine that you are chatting with colleagues during your coffee break when a recruiter comes in asking for people to work on a job for her company. All of the workers building a skyscraper downtown have just quit to work overseas. The project is in a crucial stage, and because the company is offering top pay, several of your group express interest. But when the recruiter mentions that the job requires walking along steel girders on the 30th story to carry supplies to other workers, interest wanes. The recruiter senses this and states that the pay will be $75 an hour with time-and-a-half for overtime. Some of the group groans at passing this up, but none is willing to take the job. Again the recruiter ups the offer, this time to $150 an hour. Would you be willing to take*

on the job of carrying supplies along girders far above the ground? Is there any amount of pay that would entice you to do so?

I actually have presented this little fantasy to many parent classes and found that typically if the promised pay went high enough, some parents said they would be willing to accept the job while most would not consider the job for any amount of pay. There are two points to be made from this.

There are some tasks that we are unwilling to undertake no matter what the incentive is. For example, surely none of us would intentionally endanger our children for any amount of reward.

> *In bringing up children, spend on them half as much money and twice as much time.*
>
> -Author Unknown

Other than for extreme actions that are too dangerous, too frightening, or too completely violates our values, most of us will attempt to meet challenges if enough incentive is provided. For example, a girl who always gets up late for school and who can earn a ticket to a rock concert by being ready to leave on time is very likely to be in the car long before she needs to be.

Thus, children are no different from adults in this regard, but they vary widely in how interested they are in particular choices and opportunities from those eager for anything novel to those who seem content with a few of the same old things. Since Abby seems to fit into the latter category, your challenge is bigger, but it still is to determine what will serve as an incentive for her. Meet the challenge by consciously observing her interests and how she spends her time. For example, does she like certain sports, watch a particular television program, or listen to certain kinds of music? With the answers in mind, think about what you might offer that fits with what you observed. Would she be interested in a ball to fit her sport, a toy to match a favorite television character, or a CD of a favorite singer? Or maybe she has a school friend who lives far enough away that she needs a ride to see her and you could offer a ride to the friend's house as a reward.

In addition to these ideas, remember that many children are especially eager to earn special time with parents, particularly if they are allowed to specify the activities. Here is an example of how you might offer such a reward:

CHALLENGES IN DEVELOPING A HOME PROGRAM

Planning a Sunday outing for the family (within two weeks). You can plan for up to three hours for an activity within a 30-mile drive from home and which costs no more than $20 for all of us to participate. Also, Mom and Dad must approve the plan at least three days ahead of time.

If none of these ideas solves your concerns, keep looking for alternatives. If after diligent effort you are unable to find a reward to interest Abby, she may need professional assessment to determine whether she might actually be depressed. If so, after suitable treatment she will be more able to participate fully in your home program, and identifying reward choices will be easier.

Our children like going on outings with us. However, we don't know how to handle it when one wants to trade credits for such a reward but the others either don't have the credits or don't want to use them that way.

This circumstance is rich in opportunities and you can consider a number of alternatives, including:

1   Allow the children to pool their credits to get enough for a family outing. This works well if all the children are interested in the same reward, but questions may arise. For example, does each child have to contribute an equal number of credits, or might one who wants it more or sooner put in a larger share? Also, how would you handle an older child badgering a younger one to use credits for something the older one wants more than the younger? Answering these questions ahead of time can avoid new battles. If you can work them out, this can be a viable resolution.

2   In defining the reward item, specify that this choice is available only if and when each child has earned the right number of credits and agrees to use them that way. While this can work, it could set up conflicts or disappointments if the children can't agree. The good side could be children learning to negotiate and cooperate. The down side could be added family hassles as one child presses for the others to agree. Also, any child with no interest in the reward, would, in effect, have veto power. That situation could cause enough resentment to make the item negative and not a reward at all, but if your children are good at cooperating with each other, this could work.

3   Treat each reward choice individually so that when a child earns and selects a reward, you provide it regardless of whether the other children have a similar interest. This choice can work fine and may add the special reward of time alone with one or both parents, but it also can mean added expense and time for you.

4   Make it clear that if credits are traded in for a particular outing, the child is actually choosing to treat the whole family. If you do this, include such a provision in your definition of the reward choice. For example:

Hosting a family trip to Ben and Jerry's for ice cream (within a week).

This alternative makes it clear that choosing to use credits this way amounts to a decision to share. Some children may dislike this idea and never choose it but others may enjoy sharing and work hard in order to do so. Some parents expressed astonishment that their "selfish" children have eagerly chosen such a reward. Perhaps being able to host the family gratifies a sense of importance that the child otherwise doesn't feel.

If none of your children ever selects a reward involving time with family, accept whatever they do choose and focus on the real interests of each child.

We follow your program idea, but wouldn't it be a lot easier just to give our son a certain amount of money for each thing on the list, rather than fooling around with credits?

Our society has become so commercialized that our values often are badly distorted. Halloween, once a time for clever homemade disguises, now involves elaborate decorations and factory-made costumes. Weddings often seem to be measured by the costs. Even how loved was the deceased is sometimes judged by the cost of the casket. In such a world it seems a good idea to keep rewards for your children clearly focused on their effort and its benefits, free of the slippery meanings of the monetary world.

Despite such concerns, in the reward list for Johnny Jones shown above, one choice is *"25 cents (15 cents to spend and 10 cents to save) – 100 credits."* It was included because parents sometimes ask, as you have, about incorporating monetary rewards into the overall program. This item illustrates a way to include money while assuring it is not the child's only choice. The clause about saving part of it further moderates the monetary aspect. While this is a feasible reward choice, there are a number of drawbacks to consider.

First, money is universal and children have access to it from a variety of sources. If a child gets as much money for a birthday or can find as much in the sofa as can be earned by concerted effort over days through the program, it will be difficult to make the program attractive to the child. The extra money may allow the child to achieve a desired reward with little effort and provide no sense of accomplishment to sustain continued effort in the program.

CHALLENGES IN DEVELOPING A HOME PROGRAM

Second, money also can be used in so many different ways that it could become quite difficult to associate the money earned by responsible behavior with what the money buys. In the process, the vital association between the effort and the material reward might well be confused or lost entirely.

Third, time with parents is a powerful incentive. While you could assign a monetary cost to playing catch, it seems a bit crass to have your child pay you 50 cents for special time with you.

For all these reasons, your program will be stronger if you use credits and maintain the clear connection between your child's efforts and its benefits.

This program sure is different from the way I was raised, but I'm giving it a good try. What I can't accept, though, is the money thing. I don't mind spending time with my children when they do well, but paying the children to do things that they should do really bothers me. What do you think?

This question addresses the issue discussed in the example just above, only from the opposite point of view. It is possible to construct a very effective program without compromising your comfort about "the money thing." Many of the most powerful rewards relate to privileges. One of the most important messages we can convey to our children is that freedom and choice – that is, privileges – are earned by individuals who demonstrate through responsible behavior the capacity to manage them. Among the privileges you can focus on to stay clear of money is special time with you.

To be sure that I have addressed all of your concerns, I should make one more comment. You mentioned your discomfort with paying your children to "do things they should," and of course in some sense of the phrase, the entire program involves paying (with credits) for things parents think their children should do. In part this approach is based on the observation that the way the wider world operates overall is that responsible behavior (work) results in benefit (pay). Our whole monetary system is an embodiment of the Principle of Positive Reinforcement. If you can see things in that light, you may accept that there is nothing inappropriate in rewarding children as part of teaching them to be responsible.

We have two children. Missie gets most things done easily and Marty always dawdles and fails. How can we be fair if we reward Marty for things Missie does anyway?

Many families have one child who learns responsibility easily and another who requires extra effort. This challenges parents to meet the needs of each without being unfair to either. It can be even more complicated if you feel that you must treat each child exactly the same, regardless of their differences.

> *A woman brought her identical eleven-year-old twin daughters to see me. She felt as if she were walking on a razor edge as she struggled to treat them equally all the time, fearing that any tiny false step could raise claims of favoritism. As one example, if she woke Nellie first in the morning and Ellie even a second later, Ellie claimed her mother didn't love her, much as Nellie would react if the mother started with Ellie. Nor could she win by waking them together or alternating which she woke first. This mother could not imagine giving up her struggle nor could she see that she might well be inadvertently teaching her children to feel fragile and vulnerable, though acting as if each was justified in feeling wounded when she didn't come first in every way likely did just that.*

This anecdote illustrates how detrimental it can be for children to believe that they can dictate how their parents treat them. These twins invested so much energy into assuring that they were treated with preference that they had little energy left with which to handle the challenges of the rest of their lives. One result is that they never learned to take responsibility for their own behavior, including control over their own reactions and emotions.

As you design and operate your program, keep clear in your mind that your job is to start where each child is and to help each to increase the level of responsible behavior from there. When you write your program, include target behaviors that fit each child. For example, if one child doesn't make the bed regularly, consider adding that to your program, but don't include it for the child who already does that job. Don't be surprised or annoyed if the one who already makes the bed complains, since it will not seem fair. To help the child understand, explain your reasoning. For example:

> *Missie, I'm pleased to know you are interested in how you and Marty are both doing. I can see that it seems unfair that he earns credits for making his bed and you don't. I'd wonder if I were you, too, so let me explain. Our job as parents is to help each of you learn to take responsibility for your behavior. That includes things like making your beds. We are really pleased that you learned to do this a long time ago so that you don't need our help. But as you know, Marty has a hard time getting his bed made even though he can do it when he tries. So, we put this in his program to help him get used to doing it on his own. We'll keep working with him until that happens. That is the same reason we put getting your math turned in on time in your program, to help you with something that has been hard for you even though we know you can do it when you try. We'll keep working with you until you can do this on your own, too.*

CHALLENGES IN DEVELOPING A HOME PROGRAM

Children approached with such a clear, thoughtful, and truthful explanation recognize how reasonable it is and tend to complain much less. If Missie does complain and if you think another explanation will help her understand, explain again. After that simply repeat, *"I'm sorry if you don't understand, but that is just the way it is."* Defending yourself is not a constructive response, and if you are pushed, I suggest you rely on the guidelines for tuning out persistent arguing discussed in Chapter 2.

We have three children, and it is difficult to be sure that each can earn exactly the same reward. How can we handle this?

I strongly suggest that you give up trying to provide each child exactly the same reward. Each child is an individual and is best dealt with accordingly. Explain that you are working to meet the needs of each. The rest of your message will be conveyed by how you act.

On the reward side, most children have their own interests and thus do better with reward choices that fit them. Beyond that, if your children pay attention to the number of credits each can earn, I suggest that you intentionally revise one or all of the credit structures so the numbers add up to quite different amounts. For example, you could plan on one child being able to earn 50 or so credits on a perfect day while another can earn 100 or so. If one child does not yet read you can use tokens. Of course changing the credit structure also means adjusting how many credits each would have to earn for specific rewards. It is important to be reasonably balanced from your own point of view as to how much effort each must make to get about the same level of reward, but that is something you can keep to yourself. If the child who earns fewer credits complains, you can simply point out that fewer credits are required to trade for rewards, also.

The idea is to assure that each child has an opportunity to earn desired rewards by investing a reasonable amount of effort. For children who are succeeding, how each child is doing relative to siblings will be of secondary importance.

Our twelve-year-old daughter is doing very well on the program, but lately she seems a little less enthusiastic than she was. She has earned about 2000 credits but doesn't want to trade any in because she doesn't want her total to go down, and we wonder if this could have anything to do with her losing interest. What do you think?

This is an interesting development that I have seen only a few times. Some children watch the total number of credits they earn as an index of their success, and they do not want to see their scores go down. This is an admirable reaction in that it reflects her interest in her own continuing success, but it carries with it the risk that you are seeing in the gradual lessening of her interest.

Early in the program, gains from one day and even from one week to the next were quite prominent so that acquiring ever more credits was a noticeable achievement. For example, when she went from 100 to 200 credits, it was a big thing, and even from 1000 to 1100 may have seemed an accomplishment. By the time she reached a couple thousand, adding another 100 probably had lost its sizzle. At the same time, since she is reluctant to let the number go down, she has not yet experienced the material reinforcement side of the program to boost her interest. Eventually, it is likely that she will feel no incentive at all for continuing her good progress.

Fortunately, you can deal with this situation by simply keeping two balances, one the grand total of all the credits she has ever earned and the other the balance after deducting credits for whatever rewards she chooses. That way, she can use her credits as intended in the program design while continuing to observe and enjoy her large total. Tell her how you will keep track and encourage her to trade in credits soon so that she directly experiences the reward, and you are likely to see her interest is completely revived.

Our problem is that we do lots of things together as a family and it is hard to come up with rewards which are special enough to interest the children. Do we have to stop our family activities to make this program work?

Yours is a problem most children would like their parents to have. For most families the issue is easily managed. Your challenge is to identify incentives that are interesting enough to drive your children to complete their responsibilities. Among your choices might be an item that allows a child to plan a family activity, as described earlier, since being in charge can be very rewarding to some children. Be creative and also ask your children for their ideas, and you likely will come up with very enticing choices.

If your family includes children whose behavior is extremely challenging and you cannot hit upon rewards to interest those children, you may have to take more drastic measures to assure compliance. Start by reviewing how many extras you provide your children regardless of their behavior. When you weigh how much you do for your children against the importance of needed behavior changes, you may conclude that you can better meet your overall goals by making some rewards contingent upon responsible behavior. Make sure that the children understand that in our world, benefits, including choices and privileges, are directly coupled with responsible behavior. In some families such adjustments may not improve things enough for a reasonable level of cooperation. In that case, it may be necessary to seek a family evaluation with a professional who can more directly determine what underlies the child's resistance and provide guidance for moving beyond it.

STEP 3: CHALLENGES IN MANAGING A HOME PROGRAM

Often when parents change the way they operate in their homes, children at first are left feeling uneasy. They may react in a variety of ways, typically including some testing of the new arrangements. Parents also may be uncertain about their own revised roles. The resulting pattern can produce a variety of challenges, some of them rather unusual. To help you prepare for unanticipated situations, here are some examples related to day-to-day operations of the program.

Because of our work schedules, we do not have the same times together each day of the week so there is no regular time we can set up for a daily review. What can we do?

As your question recognizes, failing to hold daily reviews can greatly undermine your program and I have stressed the importance of building them into your family life. The daily review is an essential component of the program since it ties together your expectations, the child's responsible behavior, your praise, the credits the child is earning, and the ways the credits can benefit the child. Since your schedule is so variable that you cannot follow this recommendation exactly, you will have to plan carefully to be sure you hold a review sometime each day. This will demand more discipline from you, as likely do many aspects of your complicated lives, but it can be done. Your challenge will be to adapt the guidelines presented above to your particular circumstances. As examples:

- Each day make it clear to your children when they can expect to meet with you.
- Be especially generous with on-the-spot social reinforcement whenever you know it will be extra long before your next review meeting.
- Make sure you have a way to monitor, track, and record successes, particularly for behaviors that may not be reviewed for more than 24 hours at a time.

Your program is meant to help you and your child and it is can be flexible enough to work for you in your real-world circumstances. Just remain true to the underlying principles that give the program its power while adapting the details and your operating procedures to best meet your family's needs.

We have things working pretty well, but sometimes our lives get very confusing and things come up so Kenan can't meet the criteria for an item. How can we manage when that happens so that he still has a chance?

What you describe is pretty common. While it is important to maintain the standards of the program, your home program can be adapted to meet many changing circumstances, with one important caveat:

> *Do not change your agreement in response to complaints from your child after the fact.*

> *Suppose that as you are driving Kenan home from the dentist, he realizes that it is too late for him to get his homework done on time. When he starts fussing about how unfair it is that he can't earn his credits, you recognize his point, you feel bad for him, and you are tempted to agree that he can have extra time to do his homework.*

While this sounds like a reasonable response, changing your mind to your son's fussing would teach him that fussing can pay off when things aren't going his way. Instead, tell Kenan that you are sorry he is disappointed this time but that in the future he can alert you to any similar problems and then you can plan ahead to work out a solution. Whenever either of you anticipates a legitimate complication, you can adjust your expectations so he has the opportunity to succeed. For example, during breakfast on a day with an afternoon dental appointment that will again make Kenan late for his homework, acknowledge the complication and tell him. For example:

> *Before your appointment at 3:00, we need to change thing. For today, you will be successful when you have your homework done by 7:00 p.m.*

With that consideration and plenty of time to organize himself around this modification, Kenan will have every chance to succeed. By consistently operating this way, you will teach him that with advanced planning he can expect fairness and consideration, while belated fussing will gain him nothing. Many children get good at looking ahead, and they ask for needed changes in time to avoid disappointments, good preparation for adult functioning.

Our program has gone pretty well in some areas, but now our son thinks he should get credits for everything that he does. What do we do now?

CHALLENGES IN DEVELOPING A HOME PROGRAM

A father was doing some heavy trimming in his yard, leaving piles of cuttings in his wake, when four-year-old Tyler began picking up after him. While it was common for Tyler to want to help, this time he stuck with the task and worked very hard for over an hour. While putting away the tools the father informed Tyler that he was going to give him two tokens for his great job, a bonus not specified on his chart. Tyler responded with delight, dashing in to tell his mother, showing that the reinforcement value was far greater than two tokens.

A week or so later when the father went to do some yard work, Tyler quickly came to help. Not surprisingly, he immediately asked, "Daddy, do I get extra tokens for helping this time too?" His father replied, "No, Tyler. I gave you the two tokens that one time to thank you for working so hard. But we all work together to keep our yard looking nice because we love our home and our family." Tyler thought about that for a moment and that was the last he said about it until he explained the same thing to his mother later that day. Clearly, even though he may not have liked it, he was satisfied with the explanation.

I share this story to illustrate what I think is a fair way to deal with your son when he asks to be rewarded for whatever task he completes. It is not surprising that he expects rewards for everything he does if he does not yet fully understand how the program works. Your challenge is to make it clear that each of you has certain responsibilities to the family. Explain that one of your responsibilities, as his parent, is to help him learn to do what is expected. Then remind your son that you have developed your home program to make it easier for him to learn to fulfill his responsibilities.

If your child continues to demand rewards for every deed after you have explained, review your efforts so far to be sure you have laid the groundwork well. Have you clearly conveyed your expectations and how the reward side of the system works? Have you explained, preferably not more than a couple different ways, what you will reinforce and what you won't, as well as your reasoning? If so, all that remains is to repeat that you have explained the best way you know how, acknowledge that it is too bad that the child didn't understand, and then calmly add, *"But that is just the way it is."* Then disengage, leaving it to your child to come to grips with accepting something undesirable. You cannot do that for him, but you can avoid continuing a pattern that uses up energy he could better spend by behaving responsibly.

We think we may be able to make a program work, but we know our daughter will fight it and still screw up from time to time. We are thinking it will be a good idea to "fine" her some credits when she doesn't do what she is supposed to. What do you think about that idea?

Fining children credits for failures is an approach that has been suggested by some behavioral specialists but there are several reasons I think this is not a good idea. For one, it perpetuates the notion that discipline requires making it bad for children who make mistakes. For another, for children who make a good many errors on their way to learning to behave responsibly, taking away credits for each error could mean that they never accumulate enough credits to trade for a material reward. Anyone who has had to continue making payments on a car that has long since ceased to run understands what it is like to be in such a hole. Rarely or never achieving a reward would mean that however nicely designed your program appears to be, your child really wouldn't be on a reward system. The power of the approach is in coupling material and social reinforcement with responsible behavior, and if that association never gets a chance to occur, there is no program. I strongly urge you to avoid resorting to fines for inappropriate behavior.

Chapter 6

Maintain the Program while Your Child Is Away from You

Most parents are concerned about how their children behave while away from their direct influence. Fortunately your program can help you to monitor your child and to extend your influence outside your home. To accomplish this, you need a responsible adult or trusted and mature teenager to observe and report back to you about your child's behavior when you are not there.

While the same approach can be used in settings as diverse as soccer practice, scout meetings, or sleepovers, school is more often of concern. Therefore, below are detailed guidelines for working with your child's teacher, should you and the teacher agree extra help is needed.

Note that with suitable modification, the same approach can be applied anywhere you make comparable arrangements.

Step 1: Create a Partnership with the Teacher

Remember that while your specific child is your main concern, teachers have to remain equally committed to all of their students. Therefore, whatever you ask of your child's teacher has to fit into her many duties.

Arrange to meet with the teacher to discuss your child's behavior. Tell her about your home program in enough detail that she'll understand your approach. Describe your specific concerns about your child's school behavior and performance and tell her that you would like to extend your home program to help your child become more responsible at school, by reinforcing specific appropriate school behaviors. Ask the teacher for her observations of your child and about any specific concerns she has, recognizing that she likely knows better than you can in what areas your child most needs help. By establishing a clear partnership, your joint efforts will be far more effective than anything you can do alone.

Most teachers agree to work with parents, although their levels of enthusiasm vary somewhat. Only a few times in my years of working with families did parents report that teachers refused to participate in the program. Nearly all of those, after I called to clarify the approach, agreed to do their parts.

Step 2: Develop Shared Expectations

Establish the Format

Once the teacher has agreed in principle and the two of you have agreed on areas of concern, explain to the teacher the goal of focusing your child away from inappropriate behavior and toward behaving responsibly by defining success behavior, using the same format you use at home:

"_____, *you are successful when . . .*"

Describe the three characteristics of well-worded success statements:

1. Realistically reachable goals,
2. Focused on appropriate behaviors and expressed in positive terms,
3. With criteria of success that are clear to your child, the teacher, and you.

MAINTAIN THE PROGRAM WHILE YOUR CHILD IS AWAY FROM YOU

Be aware that meeting these characteristics can be challenging for a busy teacher who may find it easier simply to tell the child to *"be good"* or *"behave"* for part or all of the day. Gently emphasize the importance of greater clarity and detail, since *"good"* provides your child almost no guide to improved behavior or a time frame for expecting to be reinforced.

Define the Content

With that preparation, you are ready to select specific behaviors to modify. Since at school, academic performance, peer relationships, and respect for authority cause the most concern, consider your child's needs in each area.

Academic performance may be addressed by defining specific levels of work on class assignments or tests. For example:

> *Morgan, you are successful when you have your math assignment turned in on time and at least 80 percent of your answers are correct.*

Note that the expected amount of work and accuracy must be realistic, based on your child's abilities and past successes. If Morgan typically fails most answers, it might be more realistic to expect as little as 25 percent correct and then to raise the level as the successes begin to mount.

Peer relationship problems can cause considerable difficulty even if a child has no academic struggles. Here is a sample item addressing such concerns:

> *Leron, you are successful when you willingly take turns while playing with the other children during recess.*

Tailor any concerns in this area to what you know about your child's struggles with peer relationships. Also make sure that there will be appropriate supervision so that accurate reports on your child's behavior can be provided to you. For example, for Leron a playground attendant would have to be available to observe and report on his successes during recess.

> *Children seldom misquote. In fact, they usually repeat word for word what you shouldn't have said.*
>
> —Author Unknown

Respect for authority is essential for children to take full advantage of the learning environment. Here is an example of a relevant item:

Sofia, you are successful when you cooperate with the teacher during reading circle.

It is important to come to an agreement with the teacher on a workable number of tasks, considering both your child's needs and the many demands on the teacher's time. Because handling a few items well is better than trying to do more than the teacher's time allows, plan on no more than three or four items in all.

STEP 3: DEVELOP A SCHOOL BEHAVIOR CHART

Once you have agreed on a set of items for the program, your next step is to develop a simple chart for the teacher to use, just as you did at home but covering fewer days of the week. A sample school chart appears here:

School Extension to our Home Behavior Program					
(Name) _____ for the week of _____ 20__					
... you are successful when:	Mon	Tue	Wed	Thu	Fri

Figure 10. Sample behavior chart for school use

A small, sturdy index card works well for this. Since you'll need a new chart each week, you might want to draw one up without the items, copy it, and then fill in copies as you need them. While some enthusiastic teachers offer to make the charts, it is best to gently decline the offer and make the chart yourself so that you don't lose any momentum in implementing the program.

MAINTAIN THE PROGRAM WHILE YOUR CHILD IS AWAY FROM YOU

STEP 4: ESTABLISH OPERATING PROCEDURES FOR SCHOOL

The final step in organizing the school extension of the program is to work out the operating procedures and to make sure that your child, the teacher, and you each understand your specific responsibilities.

First, your child is responsible to take the card to school each day and to place it wherever the teacher requests.

Second, the teacher is responsible to record the child's successes for each item on the chart by writing her initials in the appropriate place on the card. Since how the teacher carries out this responsibility can greatly impact the effectiveness of the program, keep these points in mind:

- Ask the teacher to use her *initials* since they are easy for her and do not tempt the child to fudge as check marks or entering a zero might.
- Emphasize the important of not focusing on items not completed successfully, since attention to a failure can increase the likelihood that it will occur again; instead, ask the teacher to minimize any comments and to leave a blank on the chart for any item not completed successfully.
- Encourage the teacher to keep the card free of extraneous information, including notes about misbehavior, since they could distort the success-oriented program. Ask her to communicate to you in some other fashion about concerns not addressed on the card.

Third, at the end of each school day, your child is responsible to pick up the card from the teacher, directly from her hands if possible. When the teacher passes the card indicating successes for the day to the child, the chances are very good that she will offer a smile and some praise for any successes, thus providing extra social reinforcement.

While some teachers might suggest the school card come home weekly, there is good reason to stress having your child bring it home each day.

> *A ten-year-old girl showed great and consistent improvement from her challenging behavior at home, but even a few weeks into the program her school behavior showed a confusing pattern. Review of her school cards for five weeks, when lined up for comparison, showed:*

Mondays -   *Near perfect success for all items*

Tuesdays -   *Somewhat less success*

Wednesdays -   *Little or no success*

Thursdays -   *Somewhat more success, much like Tuesdays, and*

Fridays -   *Near perfect successes, much like Mondays.*

All attempts to understand were fruitless until I learned that the child was given her school chart to bring home only on Fridays. Discussion revealed that because of some reward on the weekend, she was eager to do well at the beginning of the week, but, lacking any feedback, her interest waned by the middle of the week. Then her interests were revived as she anticipated getting her card and the extra credits she'd earned toward a reward on the coming weekend. Upon learning this, the parents and teacher agreed to change to a daily turn-around for the card, and from then on the child did very well all through the week.

Daily turn-around of the chart bypasses such problems. Further, it lessens the chances that the teacher will neglect timely completion of the chart, thereby also lessening the chances of errors in recording.

> *Don't worry that children never listen to you; worry that they are always watching you.*
>
> ~Robert Fulghum

Many parents become doubtful at about this point, sure that their children are not responsible enough to bring the card home. They note that their children lose their lunches, forget homework, occasionally come home with only one shoe, and never bring home school papers. While basing expectations on past performance typically makes sense, the school extension of your home program is different enough from other parts of your lives that such expectations may well be off target here. In practice, almost all children on this program do bring their cards home, in part at least because many of them view the card as "money in the bank," more valuable even than real money or other possessions. Even children who regularly lose their lunch money tend to get their cards home. The likely reason is that the card represents a direct link to both the material reward associated with the program (which is, at best, what money represents) and the more valued parental social reinforcement, something even money can't buy.

"Okay," you may say, *"that might be right for other people's children, but you've never met our guy. He'll never follow through."* If you remain unconvinced and concerned that your child won't bring the card home, you have a tool to remedy the situation readily at hand. Simply add an item to your home program. For example:

> *Elijah, you are successful when you bring your school card home and give it to Mom before our daily review meeting.*

The worst that can happen by adding this item is that you may end up providing reinforcement the child really didn't need, not a big thing at all.

Fourth, when the card comes home from school each day, you are responsible during your daily review to use the information from the card as a substitute for your own observations. When you are going through your home chart and you get to the school items, consult the school card, praise your child for successes, record the appropriate credits on your home chart, and continue your review as usual.

Fifth, remember that the principles underlying this approach apply to teachers as well as the rest of us. With that in mind, make it a point to reinforce the teacher for working with you on the school portion of your program. A call after the first day or two and a nice note by the end of the first week would be good ideas. After a couple of weeks, a note to the teacher's principal, with a copy to the teacher, commenting on your gratitude might be especially appreciated and therefore effective. And while you are at it, make sure that you recognize your own success in making this effective and take time to do something special to reward yourself.

It will not be difficult to apply this same approach to other situations when you cannot be with your child. Use each of the steps to establish an extension to your home program, working with whomever (coach, sitter, grandparent, neighbor, etc.) will be caring for the child, and you will be able to maintain your influence toward teaching responsible behavior wherever your child happens to be.

If a child lives with criticism, he learns to condemn.
If a child lives with hostility, he learns to fight.
If a child lives with ridicule, he learns to be shy.
If a child learns to feel shame, he learns to feel guilty.
If a child lives with tolerance, he learns to be patient.
If a child lives with encouragement he learns confidence
If a child lives with praise, he learns to appreciate.
He a child lives with fairness, he learns justice.
If a child lives with security, he learns to have faith.
If a child lives with approval, he learns to like himself.
If a child lives with acceptance and friendship, he learns to find love in the world.

~Dorothy Law Neite

Chapter 7

How to Reduce Inappropriate Behavior

All too often distraught parents ask, *"But Doctor, what do I do when . . . ?"*

> *. . . three-year-old Justine has a tantrum every time I insist she take my hand while walking in a parking lot?*

> *. . . six-year-old Kaleb grabs for things off shelves in the supermarket and then whines loudly when I don't let him keep what he takes?*

As common as they are, such situations and concerns require more than simple advice to take specific steps. Because of that, I have stressed here the development of an overall approach to proactively teaching children to assume responsibility for their own behavior.

As you know all too well, while that long-term maturational process is taking effect there are times when behaviors are so unacceptable they simply cannot be ignored and adults must intervene at once.

A word of caution: the title of this chapter may directly attract the attention of parents with children whose behavior is especially distressing. While the manner of dealing with challenging children discussed below is powerful, it can be fully effective only when accompanied by consistent positive reinforcement for appropriate behavior and by the withholding of parental response to inappropriate behavior.

Misconceptions about A Powerful Tool

Time-out is a widely used and almost as widely abused tool of discipline that serves as a powerful tool when used properly. Even if you personally have had or have observed poor results with time-out, I hope that you will read on with an open mind, since here you are likely to find concepts that are quite different from those you have heard or read before. You will learn how to bring the full power of time-out to bear on your overall efforts to teach your child responsible behavior.

Time-out is a decades-old technique that has been applied in a variety of settings by parents, teachers, and many others. While the evidence is strong that it is the most effective tool available to interrupt and eliminate inappropriate behavior, not all applications have proven successful. In fact, time-out has been so widely misused that it often has been turned into just another form of punishment with all those unfortunate implications.

> In the 1960's, investigative reporters discovered that the staff of a facility for mentally retarded individuals had cut flaps for doors in large packing crates and used them to isolate uncooperative patients, sometimes for hours at a stretch, justifying this abuse as "time-out."

Such reports tainted the whole concept, but with new guidelines to curtail abuse, the approach prevailed and remains in everyday use. Still, it is common to hear parents and other child-care workers threaten children with remarks like, *"If you don't stop that and behave, you're going to time-out!"* Such threats by their nature distort the time-out approach and throw the whole notion into a punitive context. Here I will discuss what it takes to get the best from this very important tool.

How to Apply Time-out In Your Home

The Purpose

The term time-out is short for "time out from positive reinforcement." Time-out is designed to reduce benefits to children during unacceptable behavior, specifically by withholding positive reinforcement – an important aspect of mastering the full power of the principle.

HOW TO REDUCE INAPPROPRIATE BEHAVIOR

In the context of our overall approach, time-out provides a means of stopping inappropriate behaviors when you cannot wait for the other tools in the system to have that impact. With such behaviors out of the way, the positive reinforcement program can support compatible, appropriate behavior.

THE PROCEDURE

How the time-out procedure is used determines its effectiveness. Handled badly, it can be turned into punishment, with all the negative ramifications already discussed at length above. Handled well, it can be established as a potent parenting tool for containing and eliminating your children's inappropriate behavior. To assure the constructive application of the technique, you will need fully to understand several elements.

The Test

Determine whether to use the technique simple by *telling the child to stop.* Notice that I did not say "ask" the child to stop.

> As a mother described seven-year-old Debbie as "out-of-control," the girl poked into things in the office. Several times the distraught mother meekly requested, "Please don't do that," or "Stop getting into the doctor's things, Debbie, okay?" When Debbie banged on the windows, the mother increased her pleading with the girl to "please don't hit the window" and "please stop."
>
> When the mother was advised to "Tell her to sit down in her chair," she seemed perplexed and started to again plead with the girl. Urged again to "**Tell** her to sit down in her chair," she repeated, "Debbie, sit down in your chair." Debbie looked at her mother for a moment and then immediately sat down. The relieved but perplexed mother asked, "Why did she do that?" *clearly indicating confusion about the difference between a request and a demand. Fortunately, a few weeks later she reported that Debbie was much more cooperative, a change that she attributed to her new insight and her own changed parenting style.*

Most of us, taught to be polite, feel we should ask, rather than demand, even requesting that children *"please"* stop and adding *". . .okay?"* at the end of the sentence. Either of these is seen by the child as offering a choice. While there are many times when it is appropriate to give children choices, the times when parents have determined a behavior is inappropriate are not among them.

Of course if your child stops when told to, you don't need to use time-out.

> *The clash between child and adult is never so stubborn as when the child within us confronts the adult in our child.*
>
> –Robert Brault

If your child does *not* stop, you may wish to tell the child a second time to stop. For maximum effectiveness, here is a very useful rule of thumb:

Never tell your child to "stop" more than twice before taking effective action to assure it happens, including when using time-out.

While a mother shopped in a small clothing store, her little girl tried repeatedly to get out of the stroller. When the mother noticed, she said, "Don't do that, okay?" or "Please sit down," taking no other action. When the child got free, she pushed the stroller into a clothing rack. The mother spanked the child harshly while yelling, "I told you not to get out!" Because this mother had fussed but did nothing else, the child could not know when her mother would be serious about the matter.

Parents who give more than one or two instructions to stop rarely follow-through consistently. Nor can children recognize when "warnings" might give way to action. To avoid unnecessary confusion and afford your child the best chance to meet your expectations, make it clear from the outset that what Mom or Dad says must be taken seriously when it is first said. Children simply can't learn much from rules that are enforced inconsistently.

Whether you say "stop" once or twice, if the child does not comply the test for whether to use time-out has been passed and it is time to proceed.

The Set-up

First, when applying the time-out technique, intervene before over-taxing your own patience and internal controls. Telling your child to "stop" no more than twice supports this. You can't be effective if you fuss at your child until you are upset and you end up angrily screaming, *"I told you to calm down!"*

Second, when you decide to use the time-out technique, go to your child. If you yell from another room you may not be heard or the child may recognize that you can't know for sure, and you will get little result. If you then get angry and yell louder, you may feed a power struggle, a sure way to defeat time-out. Whether you go down that path or not, you will have no way to know if the child is complying with your directive. To be effective, go to the child, go through the technique carefully, and then follow through as needed.

The first time you use time-out

To assure your family the best possible experience with time-out, arrange to use it your first time on a day and under circumstances that will have you at your best, such as a weekend when you have time and energy to devote to a complete and positive outcome. With this starting point, you will be more likely to have the necessary patience to carry out the required steps. Think of this as your project for the day, much as you might make cleaning the garage or painting a room, and be prepared to follow through as needed.

The place for time-out

Identify a place in your home suitable for time-out, a spot you can expect to support your child in calming.

> *In our home, a chair in our little-used living room became the "quiet chair," and it was used whenever one of our two sons needed time for calming. We found the term "quiet" itself to carry with it a soothing tone. (Try saying it aloud and listen to how it sounds to you.)*
>
> *Occasionally when several friends were over and play became especially active and intense, one of our sons would leave the group and sit in the quiet chair for a few minutes, as if to regroup. Each seemed to have found benefit in taking time to regain his composure, internalizing the process used to help both boys before they could do it for themselves.*

Avoid any spot in your house previously associated with angry interchanges, since it will be difficult to calm down in a punitive place.

Many experts stress placing the child in a bleak and unrewarding place, such as the corner that is the focus of so many cartoons. This notion may be a leftover from treating time-out as a milder form of punishment, when the intention was to inflict enough discomfort for the child to "get the message." Since the most effective goal of time-out is to assure that a child who is unresponsive to parental limits has a break from activities to recover composure, there may be no reason to choose a time-out area that is bleak or forbidding. In many smaller homes, a child's room may be the only practical choice, and experience shows that time-out can work very well there.

A prototype of the technique

To illustrate the constructive use of the time-out technique, consider the following prototype time-out statement to a child:

> *Ron (or Ron and Kim), I told you to calm down. I see that it is hard for you to stop right now. It's not good to be out of control, so I'm going to help you. Go to the quiet chair. Stay there until you feel calm inside. Then come back and check with me so I can know you are calm too.*

You may note that the term "time-out" is not used in this prototype statement. By itself the term means very little. And even if you have never used the term, if your child has heard it used in a threatening or negative fashion, that experience could thoroughly taint your use of the process.

While the wording used in the prototype could be adapted somewhat to your own style, it is important to preserve both the tone and the focus on your non-critical intention to support your child's regaining composure.

Of course if you have been using time-out successfully in the past, you have no reason to change what you have been doing.

The time in time-out

Many child specialists recommend that a child stay in time-out for a set time, typically about one minute per year of age, up to ten minutes or so. If you have successfully used this standard, there is no reason to change anything. Otherwise, I recommend you have the child "stay until you feel calm inside," allowing your child to determine the length based on what it takes to regain composure. For children who may need little time, insisting that they stay longer will likely be upsetting and defeat the intent of calming them. For those who may need longer to regain their composure, returning to other activities too soon will likely result in renewed disruptive behavior. Better that the child's own internal needs determine the time away from preferred activities than to rely on a arbitrary time limit that does not take the individual child or current circumstances into account at all.

Time-out with more than one child

If two or more children fail to comply when told to stop some activity, send them to separate quiet areas, preferably beyond earshot of each other, to avoid communication between them. Instead of playing police officer, judge, or jury when either child insists, "He started it," simply declare that since the children

HOW TO REDUCE INAPPROPRIATE BEHAVIOR

are unable to be together, they each must go to the specified quiet place and each must stay until achieving internal calm.

THE ELEMENTS OF SUCCESS WITH THIS TECHNIQUE

You may still see time-out as just "the same old thing" you have tried before without much success. To highlight some of the fairly subtle but significant differences between the usual interactions when parents send children to their rooms and the approach recommended here, a comparison of the two approaches is presented in the table below.

A Comparison of parenting approaches to misbehavior	
Usual practices versus	Time-out
When the child misbehaves, parents repeatedly fuss at the child, then finally react angrily.	When the child misbehaves, parents tell the child to stop, then act if necessary while they are still calm.
Parent's message to child: "*You are bad!*"	Parent's message: "*Your behavior is inappropriate.*"
Implicit message: "*I'm really angry at you!*"	Explicit message: "*I'm going to help you.*"
Implicit message: "*You are a brat and I don't want to be around you!*"	Implicit message: "*I know that you are capable of regaining control..*"
Angry instruction: "*Get yourself into your room . . .*"	Calm instruction: "*Go sit in the quiet place . . .*"
Continuing: "*. . . until I tell you to come out.*" (or for some indeterminate but lengthy amount of time).	Continuing: "*...then check with me so I can know you are calm, too*" ("*. . . and can reinforce your better control.*").
Result: Often grouchiness and nagging, lowered self-esteem for both parent and child, therefore a continuation of poor parent-child relationship, a set-up for likely replay of the pattern next time.	Result: Resolved problem, increased sense of competence and control for both parent and child, reaffirmed parent-child relationship, increased likelihood of cooperation in the future.

Figure 11. Comparing elements of typical and time-out responses to misbehavior

When a child becomes difficult to deal with, the "usual" response from parents is to ignore the behavior at first but to react angrily when it becomes annoying enough, conveying by their tone and sometimes by their words that the child is bad, a brat, and so on. They then exile the child to a corner or bedroom to, ". . . stay there until you are 18 and ready to leave for college" or ". . . stay there until I tell you to come out." Neither a long penalty nor an indeterminate one gives the child any incentive to regain control but rather either one is likely to encourage the child to sit and fume.

The overall result of the usual angry interchange tends to be a setup for a repeat hassle the next day. It tends to leave both parent and child still tense, annoyed, or angry, feeling put upon, and reactive enough to be triggered easily back to the same feelings again.

In contrast to the usual approach, in this time-out approach you intervene early while you are calm and you put the focus not on the child but on the behavior. You emphasize that you see the child as somebody who is capable of regaining control. You send the child to the quiet place with instructions to stay, not a long time or until you decide it is over but until the child feels calm inside, making it clearly in the child's best interests to become calm as quickly as possible. And when you reconnect, you have the chance to notice and reinforce behavior you most value in your child, including staying calm. The long-term result is a growing confidence for you and your child in the capacity to regain control when things get overly intense.

> *A mother's reaction to three-year-old Liam's frequent tantrums was to "finally . . . tell him to go to his room," typically having to take him there herself ". . . to get him to calm down!" She complained that, "He just follows me right back out with this big grin on his face!" When told she seemed to be doing a great job, she demanded, "What do you mean?" Reminded that her goal was to calm Liam down and that taking him to his room produced a "big grin on his face," she replied, "Yeah, but I'm not ready for him to come out yet. I'm still upset."*

This anecdote clearly illustrates the importance of responding to challenging behavior before you are upset yourself. By learning to send her child to time-out as soon as his behavior became unacceptable, this mother was able to save herself considerable distress. She also came to recognize her son's own capacity to regroup although, in reality even earlier her child apparently was more dramatic than upset.

Manage Your Child Coming Back from Time-out

When you started the time-out process, you instructed your child to remain in the quiet place and to check with you when calm. Upon return to you, your child may be in any of three states:

1. Your child clearly is still poorly controlled. Every time your child returns still noticeably intense, send the child back to the quiet place and calmly but firmly say:

    I can see you are still not calm inside. Go back to the quiet place until you feel calm inside and then come back and check with me.

Note the reference to "every time" since it is crucial that you follow through each time the child's behavior demands it.

The demeanor of the child in the second and third alternatives will look very similar and the difference will become evident only after you weigh the matter, part of the reason for instructing the child to check with you.

2. The child has made an effort at regaining composure and comes to you looking calm, but the level of control remains tenuous. Since you won't immediately know the difference, you initially will have to respond as if the child has achieved calm with some comment like:

    It's really great to have you back with the family. You seem to feel so much better now that you are calm.

This reinforces both the calmer behavior and the feelings behind it, helping the child to recognize and understand the good feelings associated with regaining internal control.

If the child who initially appeared to be calm returns to the previous misbehavior, whether seconds or minutes later, return the child to the quiet place. Here, though, your comment should recognize that both of you had reason to think the child was doing better, for example:

I could see you were trying, but now I can tell you are still having some trouble staying calm inside. Go back to the quiet place and stay until you feel really calm inside and then come back again and check with me.

Follow through as many times as necessary to assure that it is understood: the child must become calm before resuming other activities.

3   The child is completely calm and will not require a return to the quiet place. This outcome provides you a perfect opportunity to praise your child, reinforcing the capacity to regain composure free of rancor. At that point the process is over!

Follow Through, Follow Through, Follow Through

You can learn many things from children. How much patience you have, for instance.

~Franklin P. Jones

Because this new approach to dealing with misbehavior may be unsettling, your child is likely to test you, maybe even several times, while you both get used to the process. If you react by losing your patience or otherwise give up on time-out, your child will conclude that pushing the limits can deter you from your goals. While this is no more in the child's best interests than it is yours, the child will not understand this until later, when it becomes clear how much better it is than continuing the old angry exchanges. Thus, it is up to you to demonstrate that you will follow through even in the face of your child's provocations.

To follow through, return your child to time-out as many times as necessary. Early on your child may vigorously test your resolve. Be prepared to demonstrate by your actions that you will calmly and consistently follow through for as long as it takes. And take heart: typically even the most challenging children become more responsive to time-out after the first few times.

If a child complains about going to or staying in the time-out (or quiet) place, insist that the child must go. If necessary, lead your child by the hand to go to the time-out area and hold the child there, using as much restraint as – but no more than – is absolutely required to make it clear that the child must comply.

I do *not* recommend shutting or locking a child away from parents because this is too frightening for young children and too angering for older ones. With some creative planning, you may be able to restrain a younger child in a bedroom if you use an approach that maintains communication between the child and the rest of the family. Some parents use inexpensive portable gates, even one above the other to deter kids who are good climbers. Others have described securing the partly open door against a wood block or book on the floor, using a towel around the door knob so as to avoid marring the finish. The idea is to assure that the child cannot leave the room, will not be hurt, and can still sense family in the rest of the house. Just be certain to tie things securely so that there is no chance for them to slip and smash little fingers. Since an arrangement that allows the child to hear you means that you will be able to hear the child, resolve not to react to loud complaints.

If your child is large and strong and is unwilling to go to the time-out area without an unsettling tussle, consider simply deciding that time-out should be right where you are. For example, if the child is sprawled on the floor, you might say, *"Okay, I guess this is a good place for quiet time."* Send any other children away from the area and then just make sure the child stays there until calm. Turn yourself on "robot" to maintain your own calm and use only enough pressure to assure compliance. Be as firm as you must but no more forceful than required to avoid further upset.

If your child is too wild or aggressive to stay in the time-out area using these guidelines without risk of personal harm or damage to property, then you would be well advised to seek direct help from a child and adolescent psychotherapist. Whenever a child is actually willing to fight with those most needed for support, guidance, and love – whenever a child is distraught enough to risk disrupting the most important human relationships – then that child is clearly in need of – and deserves – a careful assessment and whatever treatment is found to be indicated to relieve the situation. Anything less is a formula for lasting severe unhappiness for all concerned as well as the establishment of grossly dysfunctional family relationships.

A Warning: Do not start use of the time-out techniques unless you are confident about your commitment and capacity to follow through fully. Beginning the technique and failing to follow through would simply teach your child that continued resistance and non-compliance will pay off eventually – that if a little fussing doesn't pay off, then more will. Thus, hold off on using time-out until you are sure you can follow through; you may find that you will become increasingly confident as you experience success with the positive reinforcement aspect of your home program.

Sample Family Challenges in Implementing Time-out

While the time-out concept and approach are pretty straightforward, applying them can be challenging. The following samples from other families illustrate ways to address some such challenges:

The first time that we sent our son to time-out he stayed a long time. Later he told us he didn't think he could really come out when he was ready – because we used to tell him to stay until we told him he could come out. What are your thoughts about this?

It is unlikely that your son's misunderstanding will cause any problem for him or you except that you don't have the opportunity to welcome him back to the family in a timely manner. Chances are that once your child fully understands the new arrangement, things will go fine, and you may not need to take any action. Talk with him again and stress that he is to come to you to check so that you can know when he is calm. If your son still remains confused, consider changing the time-out area to emphasize the new arrangement. When you do so, consider changing the name from "time-out" to "quiet place" or some other acceptable term, to further stress the changes. Otherwise, I think you can feel good about the fact that your son – and therefore you – are succeeding in the use of time-out.

Maya, who is eight, responds well to time-out with her dad and even with her teacher, but when I try to send her there, she whines and fusses for what seems like hours. What can I do?

When children regularly respond significantly differently from one person or situation to another, it means that they have learned that they can best meet their needs by matching their behavior to the differences in the situation. Maya appears to have concluded that calming herself works best when sent to time-out by her dad or teacher and that whining or fussing works best with you even though you surely did not mean to teach her that. As discouraging as that is, it is good that your child has demonstrated the internal resources required to regain suitable control when guided and motivated to do so.

Your challenge is to learn to guide Maya to calm herself when you send her to time-out. Review the discussion above of the elements of time-out, concentrating on how to avoid responding to whining and fussing. Once you have all that clear in your mind, observe and talk with Maya's father to determine what is different in his handling of time-out. When you know the adjustments you need to make, talk with your daughter. Tell her that you are pleased that she is doing so well with her dad and her teacher and that you are sorry that things haven't yet gone as well with you but that you intend to make some changes so that they will. Then tell her you are going to handle things differently from now on, alluding to using her dad's approach if you are comfortable with that idea. The rest is a matter of following through on what you know is required for you to be effective. Again, she has demonstrated she can respond well; therefore success is at hand.

You say it's a good idea to have a child come out of time-out when he feels calm, but we think our son should apologize when he comes out. How can we work that in?

> *The trouble with being a parent is that by the time you are experienced, you are unemployed.*
>
> ~Author Unknown

Children, as is true for adults, are not always at their best and therefore need adult supervision and guidance to foster responsible behavior. When they err, it is important that parents are there to get them back on track. The time-out approach is designed to end inappropriate behavior by eliminating inadvertent reinforcement and to allow children to regain their composure. A demand for apology in this context risks casting a negative shadow over an otherwise positive exchange. Perhaps the biggest risk is that children would recognize that they could get out of time-out by apologizing even when they don't mean it – in effect, teaching them that dishonesty can pay off.

Clearly children should come to understand that some behaviors are unacceptable. Still, there is little to gain and much to lose by making them feel bad about themselves for sometimes failing to live up to what they are learning. Apologies, then, might best be reserved for when a child genuinely feels sad or sorry for a specific behavior and can be encouraged by a parent to apologize as a way to resolve such feelings.

Whenever we send both sons to time-out because they are fighting, six-year-old Noah comes out calm a lot sooner than nine-year-old Victor and that makes Victor mad – then he fusses and whines about how unfair it is, so time-out doesn't work for us. What can we do?

It sounds as if Noah has learned how to regain calm, while Victor still sees time-out as a punishment rather than as help for him to calm down. It appears that time-out does work for you, but so far only with Noah.

Think about what might keep Victor from responding positively to time-out. For example, do you use time-out in a way that is similar to past punishment, perhaps sending him to the same spot you once sent him when you were upset? If so, consider using a different place for time-out and any other modifications that you think might help Victor understand that time-out is to help him.

After you have reviewed your procedures, have a talk with Victor when he is calm. Explain to him that you are sorry things have not gone as well as either of you would like. Then describe to him the changes you will make so that he can get a fresh start the next time he can't calm himself. Restate the overall idea of time-out, namely to assist him in regaining calm, the same as for Noah. Point out that how rapidly each of them calms is not up to you but is up to each of them, and point out that he will probably be more successful if he concentrates on recovering his composure sooner rather than later. Take care here not to make comparisons between the boys since doing so could feed his resentment and weaken the impact of your talk.

These adjustments will assure that you have established the conditions for Victor's success with time-out. When you next use it, go through the steps carefully, and when each son comes to let you know he is calm, reinforce him for that and let him continue with other activities. Just be sure that whichever child becomes calm first stays away from the one still in time-out until both are calm and are ready to be together.

These steps will assure that you have done what you can to improve Victor's capacity to respond constructively in time-out. The rest is up to him.

During this process it is important that you avoid responding to further whining or fussing. However reasonable your argument, trying to convince Victor it is fair for Noah to move out of time-out before Victor is also ready is unlikely to succeed. Instead, just allow the storm to run its course so that Victor sees that fussing gains him nothing while regaining calm can end the problem. Thus, whenever he fusses, wait it out, and when he finally calms, reinforce him for being calm. With these changes, your chances of helping Victor to become as responsive to time-out as is his sibling are excellent.

Our child seemed to have lots of tantrums before we started time-out and is doing a lot better. Now, when we do send him to time-out, he stays there for a long time, and when we check on him, he's reading or playing by himself. What should we do about this?

My first instinct is to suggest you congratulate yourself on a job well done. I'll try to do better than that, but it is a legitimate response since it sounds as if you have helped your child regain control, a great achievement, especially for a child prone to frequent tantrums. About all that might be improved would be for the child to come to you to tell you that he is calm, and maybe he somehow missed that part of the instruction. If you think that could be true, gently

HOW TO REDUCE INAPPROPRIATE BEHAVIOR

tell him again, perhaps stressing that you want him to come to you at the end of time-out so that you, too, know how well he is doing.

There is a chance that your son is aware of your expectation but doesn't choose to come to you. That could happen if he is not truly and completely at ease inside himself. To the extent that this is true, it would be appropriate to respect the child's need for the longer time and simply let him make use of it. A child with a history of tantrums may have been caught up in power struggles and may harbor residual anger that he is gradually working out during these times, a constructive development if true. Since you can't know about for sure what is going on inside him, I would suggest that you allow the child to work out whatever he needs to by giving him the time he needs.

On the other hand, if your child tends to stay in time-out impossibly long and inconveniences other family members, you likely will need to set some kind of limit on how long you let the process go on. Without knowing your child, it is impossible to suggest an exact time-frame, but perhaps you could decide to allow the child to stay alone where he is for a half-hour after he appears to be calm, as best you can judge that. That would allow considerable time for completing his internal calming but still would give you a time when you could expect him to participate in other family activities. If you elect to use such a guideline, try the idea once to see how it works. If you see signs that the child is edgy or loses his cool unduly rapidly, then maybe you should allow a longer time alone in time-out. Whatever way you go, you deserve to feel good that you and your child have already made so much progress.

When my children are bickering and I send them to time-out, they each start blaming the other and telling me it's unfair to be sent when the other is at fault. What do I do?

What you are describing is likely just an extension of the way the children relate in other circumstances, probably including those that lead you to send them to time-out. Clearly, the children are treating time-out as a punishment, and this negative flavor undermines the effectiveness of the technique.

Tell your children again that you send them to time-out to assist them in calming when they seem unable to relate appropriately to each other on their own. Add that you are not interested in who started or did what but rather in doing your part when it is hard for them to work things out themselves. Your children may not really believe you, particularly if you have typically engaged in debates about who is at fault. To break the old pattern, stay away from that issue and restate that each of them is responsible to regain calm. Over time each child will come to recognize the advantages of regaining calm sooner rather than later and rather than arguing. Be prepared for one child to get the message more quickly than the other, a problem addressed in a previous example. Of course, it is also important that you separate the children while they are in time-out and that you have them as far out of earshot of each other as your home allows.

Since we have been sending our son to time-out instead of yelling at him, he has started saying insulting things, and that simply isn't acceptable. What do we do about this?

This unsettling behavior represents a direct test of your overall program since anything you do in response to this provocation carries the risk of reinforcing the very behavior of which you disapprove. Remind yourself that however hateful sounding the child's comments are, he is still the son you love, and he loves you – though at the moment he almost surely isn't feeling it. It is equally certain that anything you say to him when he is insulting you will give him a sense of satisfaction and thereby make him more likely to do it again. Since this sounds like a power struggle, a review of the discussion about control struggles in Chapter 4 might be useful.

Beyond that, make sure that you are calm when you send your son to time-out so that you are in no way modeling his negative reactions. Once he is in the quiet place, "turn yourself on robot," in the process withdrawing your emotions from the child for the moment. You can think about where you wish you were, fantasize about your ideal vacation, or whatever, so that you aren't attending to the child's comments. If you do not respond, the child almost certainly will run down and eventually will stop, allowing him to calm more completely. Once that happens, you will have the opportunity to reinforce him for being calm.

I urge you, though, to stifle your likely inclination to lay a huge lecture on him at that point. By giving in to that urge, you would alert the child to how reactive you really are to his tirades. That is the opposite of what you want him to learn, which is that regaining his composure more quickly will meet his needs best. Be prepared for this pattern to repeat itself a number of times since it likely has been heavily learned, but over time you may well find both the intensity of the reactions and how long they last will diminish noticeably. At that point you'll be able to congratulate yourself for lovingly assisting your child to responsible behavior in the face of substantial challenge.

How to Apply Time-out Outside Your Home

Even after achieving success with time-out at home, many parents report difficulty in applying it away from home. Why the difference? Children are good at recognizing when we are especially likely to "give in" to them, and most parents are a bit wishy-washy when children test our limits where others may see our responses. As a result, even children who do very well at home may whine for a treat at the mall or complain in a restaurant.

Since you are more likely to succeed with time-out away from home after you have achieved consistent compliance with it at home, wait to use it elsewhere until you are confident of the response at home. Then both you and your child will understand how it works and know what to expect. Because each situation calls for somewhat different preparation, I will discuss effective steps for dealing with children who typically cause significant challenges to their parents during shopping at a supermarket, eating dinner in a sit-down restaurant, and during car trips. While these are the situations parents express most concern about, the approach can be adapted to other situations as the need arises.

To assure the best possible outcome, set the stage as constructively as possible. The process will go most smoothly if you think of your effort as your special project for the day, giving it precedence over whatever else you might accomplish along the way. And it is a good idea to start with both you and your child rested and in a good mood.

While Shopping

Parents often complain about their children's challenging behaviors while they are shopping in supermarkets or other large stores, counting it among their most frustrating experiences with their children.

Basic Preparation

Set the stage for a constructive outing by anticipating possible complications. For example, expecting to shop for a week's groceries during the same shopping trip when you first try time-out away from home might well make it difficult to be as patient and effective as you need to be. Similarly, avoiding filling your shopping cart with perishables will lessen your potential stress should you have to leave your cart to tend to your child.

HOW TO RAISE DISCIPLINED AND HAPPY CHILDREN

Accentuate the Positive

I delayed my entire discussion of time-out until after talking about the reward side of the program because time-out makes the most sense and is most effective and powerful as a support when children also have learned the benefits associated with behaving appropriately. In keeping with this, follow these steps:

1. Think about the behaviors that typically trouble you when you take your child to the supermarket with you.
2. Identify behaviors that you consider appropriate and which are directly incompatible with those that concerned you during recent shopping trips with your child.
3. Write a few specific items to guide your child to behave appropriately, using the familiar format, "*, you are successful when . . .*" Here are some examples:

    . . . you sit calmly in the cart for five minutes (or . . . for one aisle).

    . . . you help Mommy spot five items on the shopping list.

4. Make sure that each item is realistically reachable, that it specifies what the child is to do (i.e., is positive), and that it is very clear.
5. Base the target length of time that your child must carry out a specified task on past experiences to assure that the child will succeed more than a third of the time. For some children, it may be necessary to set a very short standard, even just a minute or so. Some children may even require praise for sitting still in the cart ten steps into the store. If so you might say *"It sure is nice shopping with you when you stay so calm."* A useful motto here is "Catch them being good."
6. Make and bring with you a simple chart for use just for this trip, listing the target behaviors and whatever number of tokens or credits you assigned to each. If your child is young enough for tokens, bring some with you and provide the child with a small bag to carry those earned.

Carry out Your Plan

Reinforce the child when the first and each additional standard is reached. For example:

HOW TO REDUCE INAPPROPRIATE BEHAVIOR

Melba, it is really nice shopping with you today. You've been calm for five minutes and already you've earned a token you can use for some special prize if you want to.

For each success by a young child, hand the earned token to the child but also mark it on your chart. For each success for an older child, mark the chart appropriately and tell the child what you have done. Continue to praise your child for being cooperative as soon and as regularly as necessary to promote continued appropriate behavior.

Check for the Need for Time-out

Some parents using these steps for the first time during shopping are surprised that their children cooperate throughout the trip and that they have no reason to use time-out, a tribute to the power of positive attention to such behavior. For less cooperative times, here are the steps to follow:

At whatever point your child loses control, as you define it, tell the child what you expect. This should not be a request but rather a clear demand from you to the child. For example:

Marcel, keep your hands on the shopping cart rail.

If the child complies, continue shopping as before. After a few seconds, for a young child, to a minute or so, for an older one, praise the child's calm demeanor. For example:

Wow, Marcel, it's fun to shop with you when you are so cooperative.

Refrain from comments such as "Marcel, it's great that you stopped grabbing things off the shelf," since you would risk teaching your child that stopping inappropriate behavior is how to get praise. After all, one can stop a behavior only if it has been started, not a notion you want to foster.

When Time-out is Required

If your child does not comply when told to do so, use the time-out procedure. Without further comment, as calmly as possible, push your shopping cart to the side and take the child out of the store. Typically the most practical choice will be to take the child to your car, but an isolated area nearby might work as well.

Put the child in the car or nearby in a safe place. If you use the car, be sure to keep the keys in your possession to assure that the child cannot be locked in with you locked out. Express the time-out message clearly. For example:

Jose, I told you to calm down in the store. I see that you can't right now. It's not good to be out of control like that, and I'm going to help you. Sit there quietly and stay there until you feel calm inside. When you feel calm, tell me so that I'll know you are calm, too.

Interact as little as possible until your child reports feeling calm. Restrain a child who tries to leave with as much force as required for compliance while avoiding a control struggle. Turn your face away and your mind on " robot" so that you can do what you must without becoming emotionally caught up in conflict. (See Chapter 5 to review more information on this.)

> *The quickest way for a parent to get a child's attention is to sit down and look comfortable.*
>
> −Lane Olinghouse

Once the child declares calm and you are convinced, return to the store and continue your shopping. With luck, you may find your cart so that you can pick up where you left off. Continue to reinforce each success for your child while refraining from mentioning earlier misbehavior since any lecture at that point will only reinforce what you don't want the child to do.

If the inappropriate behavior recurs, again tell your child what you expect and if there is no compliance, use the time-out procedure the same as before. Do this *as many times as necessary* to complete your planned shopping.

If you have had to interrupt your shopping several times to take your child to time-out, you likely will be frustrated and you may find it difficult to reinforce the child for whatever successes you observe. Please keep in mind that suitable praise for whatever cooperation occurred will provide the basis for future improvements and follow through as fully as possible.

If, on the other hand, you have completed your shopping with your child mostly cooperating, you are in a great position. Comment on the way home about how nice it was to shop together. Also comment on the credits the child earned in the store. You can mention how pleased that others, such as the absent parent and the grandparents, will be to learn what a good time you had. And you can reinforce all of this during your daily review. Further, before the next trip you can review how well things went during the last trip to the store. These are the building blocks of responsible behavior.

HOW TO REDUCE INAPPROPRIATE BEHAVIOR

Some Potential Complications

It is not uncommon for children being taken to time-out in public to protest loudly, bringing unwelcome attention to parent and child and challenging even the most dedicated parents' resolve. If you use time-out in public, you are likely to encounter some well-meaning but uninformed passers-by who will frown and even comment critically about what you are doing. Should you face such potentially embarrassing circumstances, keep your own goals clear and remember that you are providing a loving and necessary life lesson about behavior in public. You need apologize to no one for such an effort.

While most parents report good success with this approach, occasionally one will describe a child who challenges far beyond the parent's patience. If during time-out this happens to you and if after ten or fifteen minutes you find yourself getting upset with no signs that the child will regain control, take the child home without further comment. Avoid showing anger since this will reinforce the child's sense of control. When you get home, calmly restate the time-out message and send the child to your typical time-out location. Note that this is not suggested as a good outcome but rather is intended to minimize the negative impact on the child's future behavior.

AT A SIT-DOWN RESTAURANT

Another setting that parents often find difficult is a sit-down restaurant with delays to be seated, then to be served, and then to eat in contrast to more child-friendly fast-food places. All the principles discussed so far apply here just as they do during shopping.

Basic Preparation

Anything that will make you more upset if your child doesn't cooperate will undermine your effectiveness. Think of this as an opportunity to teach your child an important lesson for life so that your focus is on that outcome rather than on the meal itself or on the occasion or the company with you. You must be ready to respond as required by the child's behavior unconstrained by the reactions of others or by your own hopes for the evening.

The first time you take a challenging child out to dinner, plan ahead to assure pay off from your efforts. Start well rested so that you can be patient. It is probably best to take only your child or your child and siblings to minimize distraction from your goal. If you do include others, be sure that they will respect your efforts and your approach. Grandparents, who might suggest,

"Oh, don't be so harsh; he's only a baby," will not be helpful. Therefore ask everyone not to comment when you deal with your child.

Plan your first meal out using this approach when you will not be disappointed if things don't go smoothly or if the dinner is disrupted for a time. For instance, a special dinner out for your tenth anniversary would not be a good time to start using time-out. Since you may have to leave the table to use time-out, choose a meal that won't be spoiled by sitting a few minutes, as might happen with dishes that must be either piping hot or cold to enjoy.

Accentuate the Positive

Recall the basics of our overall approach, namely eliminating benefits of inappropriate behavior and making it good for children to behave appropriately. To apply these notions to dining out, follow these steps:

1. Before you leave home, identify the success behaviors that are most likely to help your child get through the meal calmly, remembering to focus on those that you value and that are directly incompatible with the behaviors you are concerned might occur. Also make certain that each item defines a behavior that is realistically reachable by your child and that the wording is clear. For example:

   Kelly, you are successful when you keep your voice calm for ten minutes during dinner.
   Kelly, you are successful when you calmly sit in your chair at the table for ten minutes.

   The amount of time specified should be based on how your child has done in the past in similar situations, making sure your standards are realistically reachable for your child.

2. Prepare a simple chart with the target behaviors and with a place to record successes. Be sure you have it with you and show it to your child when you arrive in the restaurant.

3. Because sitting quietly in a restaurant can be boring for a child, bring a few activities for your child to use at the table. A pad of paper and a few crayons or a small and quiet hand-held game can entertain a child for a good deal of time without disrupting adult conversation, all the more so if you occasionally show interest in the child's play.

HOW TO REDUCE INAPPROPRIATE BEHAVIOR

Carry Out Your Plan

Now you are ready to venture into the restaurant to begin teaching your child how to deal with a situation requiring restraint and cooperation:

1. Soon after arriving, and from time to time thereafter, comment on how nice it is to be eating out together.
2. Make waiting easier by providing appropriate activities and by occasionally interacting with the child about them, assuring the child suitable attention during appropriate behavior.
3. Track your child's success in meeting your identified target behaviors. Comment on each success and credits earned, then mark it on your card. Put a token directly into the hand of a younger child. Continue in this fashion throughout dinner.

Check for the Need for Time-out

If your child behaves unacceptably, quietly but firmly tell the child to change to behavior you consider acceptable. (Remember, don't ask; tell.)

If the child complies, after a few seconds for a young child or a couple minutes for an older one, praise the current appropriate behavior. Avoid comparisons with the just-stopped inappropriate behavior, which would actually reinforce *stopping* the inappropriate behavior, since the only way the child can repeat that reinforcement would be to start the inappropriate behavior again. Continue through the meal as before.

When Time-out is Required

If your child does not meet your standards use the procedure as with shopping, except for a few specific considerations:

Take the child calmly from the restaurant to your car (being sure to keep control of the keys yourself) or other suitable quiet and isolated area and state the time-out message

> *Kahil, I told you to calm down in the restaurant. I see that you can't right now. Since it's not good to be out of control like that, I'm going to help you. Sit here quietly and stay here until you feel calm inside. When you do, tell me so that I'll know you are calm, too.*

Once the child has calmed, likely rather quickly since most children really like to be inside, go back to your table and resume the meal. If the child stays calm, after a few seconds for a young one or a minute or two for an older one, comment on how nice it is to be in the restaurant together. Continue to follow your plan of rewarding all successes.

It is crucial that you follow through as many times as required and that you remain as calm as possible while doing so. Each time behavior becomes unacceptable, return the child to time-out. If you begin losing your patience, remember that it is a loving thing to teach your child to behave appropriately in a setting that will be visited many times over the years. Note also that children must learn to tolerate many similar situations, however tedious they may be, and that this is preparation for many of them. Also be prepared to ignore the disapproving reactions of others who don't know your child or your challenges but who may feel they would handle it all better.

Should you find yourself really annoyed with your child's behavior, you may not feel like praising small successes, a perfectly natural reaction. Unfortunately, but in reality, it is precisely at times like these when the most discipline is required of you. This approach requires consistently demonstrating to your child that cooperation merits social and material reinforcement – for as long as it takes for the behavior to become internalized. Since you also operate on the Principle of Positive Reinforcement, make a point of rewarding yourself for meeting these challenges despite your frustration.

In the Car

While learning how to handle inappropriate behavior in a store or a restaurant provides a useful model for many other situations, challenges posed by taking children in a car are different enough to warrant separate attention. Riding for any great distance can be tiresome to children, and confinement in a seat belt can be very distressing to an active youngster. In addition, children seem to recognize that parents are usually focused on the road rather than on them. Together those circumstances can make traveling a very tedious business for all concerned – and sometimes dangerous as well.

Fortunately, with preparation and use of time-out, children typically learn to behave appropriately, even on lengthy car trips. Parents often report that their children are more responsive to time-out in this environment than when they are home, some possible reasons for which I'll discuss below.

HOW TO REDUCE INAPPROPRIATE BEHAVIOR

Basic Preparation

All of the principles and concepts discussed so far for the home program and the time-out procedure apply here. The following represent specific aspects to consider the first time you use this approach with your child in the car:

Make sure that you are well rested and able to be patient. For best results on your first trip using time-out, plan a destination of no more than minor importance. If you are on your way to a crucial appointment, it will be difficult to meet your child's challenges calmly and patiently. Similarly, don't attempt this for the first time on your way to some place your child dislikes, such as the dentist, since that could make everything more difficult.

Bring a few small activities that the child can use while buckled in the car seat. Older children can be encouraged to bring things for themselves. As in the restaurant, a stiff pad of paper and a few crayons or a small hand held puzzle can entertain a child for a good deal of time, especially if you make a point to comment positively on what the child is doing. For example:

> *Sally, I can hardly wait to see what you are drawing. I hope you'll show me when we stop at the mall.*

Plan your route to drive on uncrowded streets so that if you have to stop the car, you can do so quickly and safely. Do not take with you anyone whom you can expect to defend your child's behavior since this will reinforce poor behavior and undermine your efforts.

Accentuate the Positive

As in all settings, be sure you clearly state your expectations and praise your child's cooperation so that time-out is less likely to be needed.

1. Before leaving home, identify how you want your child to behave in the car, focusing on specific and realistically reachable target behaviors that are directly incompatible with past misbehavior in the car. For example:

   > *Tyrell, you are successful when you sit calmly in your car seat with your seat belt fastened for five minutes while Mom is driving.*

   Set the required times to be realistically reachable for your child, taking into consideration past behavior and the length of your trip.

2. Prepare and take a card with the target behaviors listed and with space to record successes. If you are driving and can't immediately record successes,

be sure to remember them. If available, a passenger can record for you. Praise your child for each success. For example:

Tyrell, it's nice to go to Grandma's with you when you are so calm. Already you've earned ten credits!

Carry Out Your Plan

With this preparation, you are ready to go, but because driving is such an important activity, taking extra care will assure you success. Important considerations are spelled out here:

1. Do not start the car until the child is buckled in. Plan to use time-out at the outset if the child whines or resists. Similarly, if the child gets out of the seat while you are moving, find a safe place to stop immediately. Turn off the engine, secure the keys, and do not move the car until the child is properly restrained by the seat belt.
2. Once you are all buckled in and on your way, remember to comment on how nice it is to be driving with your child.
3. Each time the child meets your standards for success, comment on how good that behavior is and mention the credits earned toward some reward. Proceed on your way.

Check for the Need for Time-out

If your child should begin to misbehave according to the standards you have set for the car, tell the child what behavior you expect. (Do not ask; tell!).

If your child complies, a bit later comment on the appropriate behavior and on how nice it is to be together. Continue carrying out your plan as before.

When Time-out is Required

If your child does not comply or immediately resumes the misbehavior, quickly stop the car in a safe place. Turn off the engine and take the key so that, should you get out of the car for any reason, there is no risk of the child locking the doors with you outside. Express the time-out message:

Tyrell, I told you to calm down while we were driving. It is dangerous to drive when there is extra noise and disruption in the car. I see that you can't calm yourself right now so I'm going to help you. We will stay here with the car stopped while you quiet yourself. Stay in your seat (Or Get back in your seat and stay there) until you feel calm inside. When you do, tell me so that I'll know you are calm, too. Then we can start up again.

Some parents prefer to step out of the car and open the door on the passenger's side, both to be away from the child and to be ready to get in next to the child if misbehavior escalates. If you do that, be alert, and if possible, lock the door on the street side to assure the child is safe. Do not interact with the child, either pleasantly or angrily; avoid showing annoyance at such a time, since that is more likely to reinforce the inappropriate behavior than to reinforce the behavior you want from the child.

> *Too often we give our children answers to remember rather than problems to solve.*
>
> ~Roger Lewin

Note that if there are two children in the car and if both are involved in the ruckus, either directly or indirectly, give them both the time-out message. Remove one child from the car with you and have that child stay close at hand. Avoid interacting with the child outside the car since doing so could evoke cries of favoritism and further the disruption. Do not provide any reinforcement to either child during time out. Try practicing "turning yourself on robot."

Once the child or children have calmed and are safely buckled in, start up the car and proceed as before. After a short time of calm, comment to the child or children about how good it is to be calm and about how much you enjoy traveling together. Do not comment further on the disruptive behavior, even for comparison.

If your child loses control again, as you define it, immediately stop the car as before and go through all the same steps. To the extent possible, keep yourself calm and focus on the goal of teaching your child an important behavior change.

As with all uses of time-out, remember that follow through is critical. Accordingly, consider carefully whether you will be able to follow through long enough to assure that your child is cooperating in the car. If you aren't sure you can make it work, I urge you not to start since using the procedure without completing the process will teach the child that if a little fussing doesn't work, then maybe a lot will.

Children seem to hate sitting still in a stopped car even if they don't particularly like the destination. As a result, stopping the car and turning off the engine by themselves have a significant impact on how ready most children are to calm themselves. If you avoid giving them further reason to challenge you, you can expect fairly rapid changes. Time-out in the car seems to be effective more quickly and thoroughly than it is in some other settings for those who are consistent with their follow-through.

A Family Issue to Avoid

You stressed that our son should sit in his car seat but he likes to lay in the space behind the van's back seat with his toys. What's wrong with that?

In the U. S. children must be buckled into age-appropriate car seats. While consulting on hospital pediatric wards, I had several saddening experiences with families whose children were badly injured and, in a couple of cases, killed in auto collisions. In each case, the child was not buckled into a car seat. All of those who survived were left with limited capabilities and years of misery.

It did not matter where in the car the children started. If they were not restrained, they were battered as they struck other objects. On two occasions the children had been standing in the front seat when the collision occurred. One of these involved a bump of the car in front soft enough to barely dent the bumpers on both cars; however, both children smashed into the windshield and both ended up with severe brain damage. Both, after healing on the outside, looked like the beautiful little children they had been, but neither was responsive to the outside world in any meaningful way.

The parents involved in these cases reported tearfully that their children had refused or objected to staying in their car seats. All were equally sure nothing serious would happen to their children. Yet they were living a parent's ultimate nightmare. I needn't tell other parents how these parents felt as they beheld the damage to their precious children. These children paid enormous prices for the "freedom" to sit as they pleased in the car. My hope is that no other child ever suffers the same fate and that no other parent lives the lifetime of regret and pain that goes with it.

The program presented here includes tools necessary to assure your child's compliance and therefore safety. While sitting buckled in a car seat may be a bit inconvenient, it is easy to provide a comfortable, safe seat and easy access to toys. Even lengthy family trips can be enjoyable with suitable preparation. A sturdy box filled with a selection of safe toys and games and placed in a middle seat for use as a table for joint play can help entertain children for many otherwise tedious hours of driving. The key is for parents to take seriously their role in protecting their children so that travel can stay a healthy, happy, conflict-free experience.

> *Life affords no greater responsibility, no greater privilege, than the raising of the next generation.*
>
> —C. Everett Koop

Chapter 8

Monitor, Maintain, and Adjust Your Home Program.

By now you have learned:

- How children learn to take responsibility for their own behavior,
- How your actions – intentional or otherwise – contribute to that process.

You also have learned the practical application of your expanded understanding in order to:

- Support your child's appropriate behavior by proactively structuring a simple program for your own home,
- Extend your influence over your children even when you are not with them by enlisting the support of trusted monitors,
- Reduce the occasional inappropriate behavior that appears while you teach your child to behave responsibly, by effective use of time-out, and
- Incorporate all of this into your family life with a minimum of disruption and a maximum of benefit.

After you have operated your home program for a while, you will notice more progress on some target behaviors than others. You may have already undertaken some fine-tuning on the less effective items. As you settle into a workable routine, you may find that your child regularly completes at least an item or two. Good for your child! And good for you for setting things up to support this change! Better still, you may find that your daily reviews have led to warm and pleasant family interactions each day.

Early successes may tempt you to take your child's improved compliance for granted and to slack off on the program. While this seems natural, it can undermine and even destroy your good work. Until the appropriate behavior has been internalized – that is, has become self-reinforcing – your child will revert to the old behavior if you discontinue the promised social and material rewards. Prematurely assuming complete success is among the most common reasons for failure of positive reinforcement programs.

This inherent risk highlights a significant challenge. How do you know when your child has been reinforced enough to achieve mastery of a behavior? The answer is not so obvious since the child's behavior is likely to look about the same during the later stages of when reinforcement is still needed and after it no longer is needed.

Fortunately, there are specific steps you can take to review your progress and determine whether your child has achieved mastery and no longer requires continuing reinforcement. For most children and for most behaviors, this stage is unlikely to occur for at least a few weeks; for some children and some behaviors, it could be a good deal longer.

Review Progress and Adjust Your Program

Consider Your Impressions

Start your formal appraisal of your program by considering your overall impressions. A few weeks after you have settled in with your program, ask yourself what you *think* and how you *feel* about how your child is doing on the program. For example:

> *What were our main concerns and what were our goals when we started our home program?*
>
> *Overall, are things better in our home than when we started?*

MONITOR, MAINTAIN, AND ADJUST YOUR HOME PROGRAM.

Has our child's behavior improved in some areas but is still no better in other areas, compared to when we started?

Have our concerns about our child lessened enough to give us more peace of mind?

To gain perspective on how you are doing, compare the way things were in your family at the start and how they are now, item by item. Ask yourself what seems to be the reason for any changes that you have noticed.

When parents see changes in their children, they sometimes conjecture, *"Maybe Luis just grew out of it,"* or *"Maybe Kayla is just being nicer because Christmas is coming,"* or *"It could just be Zoe got to spend the summer with Grandma."* Parents sometimes have called me long after we worked together on a home program, again concerned about their child's behaviors. Typically after some success the parents had begun taking their child's better compliance for granted, assuming other reasons for the change and not even thinking of restarting their home programs. While extraneous circumstances can have an influence, beware of too readily discounting the benefits of your program since you risk devaluing the very factors that accounts for your child's improvements. Fortunately, in many of these cases, simply restarting a newly-focused program was all that was needed to turn things around to the parents' satisfaction. Remember that the Principle of Positive Reinforcement impacts us and our children all the time, whether or not we pay attention to it; better we be aware and harness its considerable power than to be inattentive and therefore passively subject to what can be very negative consequences.

Considering your impressions first will provide you perspective on your whole effort. Even if your chart shows success, if you sense little overall improvement, you will need to make changes. Or, this exercise may bring to light progress that you hadn't even noticed in your busy life despite real changes that show up on the chart. Either way, it is important to go on to the detailed evidence from your charting of your child's progress.

ASSESS YOUR CHARTS

When you have several weeks' worth of experience and charts, begin your first assessment of how far your child has come toward mastering one or more behaviors. Arrange your charts on a table from left to right so that you can read across from week to week for each item. If you have made changes while fine-tuning, take care in looking across the row of charts to stay with the same item. With the charts ready for easy viewing, examine the charts for trends showing improvement, lack of movement, or decline.

Below is a sample from our mythical Johnny's charts for just one item across six weeks. The results for the six consecutive weeks are lined up here in six rows just for convenience and ease of discussion. For purposes of this illustration, Johnny was responsible to take the trash out every day of the week. Before you read further, please spend a moment looking over these results and getting a feel for how to understand them. What do you notice about how Johnny is doing, based upon the record for this one item over six weeks? Once you have your own thoughts in mind, read on.

Item	Week	Mon	Tue	Wed	Thu	Fri	Sat	Sun
"Johnny, you are successful when you have the trash out of every room in the house by 5:00 p.m."	1	10	x	10	x	x	x	x
	2	x	x	10	x	x	x	x
	3	x	10	x	10	10	x	10
	4	x	10	10	x	10	x	10
	5	10	x	x	10	10	x	x
	6	10	10	10	10	10	x	10

Figure 12. Sample of Johnny's progress on one item over a period of six weeks

Week 1 shows that Johnny got the trash out on time on Monday and Wednesday. Whether that represents any change or not depends on how often Johnny had done the task before the program was started. If he never did it, two out of seven seems promising. On the other hand, if he typically did it two or three times a week, this doesn't show any progress – yet.

> *If your parents didn't have any children, there's a good chance that you won't have any.*
>
> —Clarence Day

Week 2 shows Johnny succeeding only on Wednesday, a decline from the previous week and surely not what his parents had hoped for. While it would be easy to be discouraged, this is a new program and both Johnny and his parents are getting used to the new system. Johnny may not yet be invested in earning credits because he doesn't fully appreciate the way the program will work. Maybe the parents haven't yet completely given up occasional negative responses that fulfill some of Johnny's needs for attention even without complying with the reward program. Or maybe they haven't followed through each day with the daily review, the component that ties all the elements together. Whatever the cause, there is not yet reason for alarm so early in the program.

Week 3 provides more reason for optimism. That week Johnny succeeded on Tuesday, Thursday, Friday, and Sunday, four of seven days, a nice doubling of successes from the beginning week. That surely is what Johnny's parents were looking for, but may or may not be an ongoing trend.

Week 4 Johnny again succeeded on four days: Tuesday, Wednesday, Friday, and Sunday. What do we make of that? It doesn't show any improvement over the previous week, but that week showed a doubling of the first week, and maybe holding his own for a week is good enough. Investors watching the stock market are pleased with no change after a day of dramatic increases since it bucks the trend for what went up to go down. So far so good.

Week 5 shows Johnny got the trash out on time on Monday, Thursday, and Friday, three of seven. This represents a bit of a decline from the previous two weeks but still is above the starting week, and only one fewer than Weeks 3 and 4. The overall trend continues to appear promising.

Week 6 on Johnny's chart shows that he met expectation every day but Saturday, a whopping six of seven days. It will take a few more weeks to be sure if this trend will hold up, but so far Johnny appears to be on track and there is plenty of reason for optimism.

But is there anything else we can learn from looking at Johnny's chart over this six-week period? Likely you will notice, as did at least one parent in every class of whom I asked the same question, that Johnny never succeeded on Saturday even during the last week when he got the trash out on time every other day of the week. What can be made of that observation? While there could be several explanations, only the parents, by observing and talking with Johnny, could find the answer.

Perhaps Johnny had a baseball game each of those Saturdays, and perhaps the games ran long enough that when he came home all sweaty and still pumped up, it was difficult for him to focus on his chores. Or maybe he actually got home too late to be able to get done by 5:30 p.m. Or perhaps he often went away with friends or even a non-custodial parent many Saturdays so that his routine didn't allow him to get the trash out on time.

With some thought and discussion, the parents are likely to be able to identify whatever factors are at play. Once they have done so, they might elect to modify the program in some way to support Johnny in succeeding on Saturdays also. For our above example, the chart might be amended to say something like:

> *Johnny, you are successful when you have the trash out by 5:30 p.m., except on Saturdays, when you have until 7:00 p.m. to be done.*

The idea here is to recognize legitimate barriers to success and act accordingly. Remember that this whole approach is intended to help you to help your child assume appropriate levels of responsibility. The structure is to support your efforts to get to your goals and therefore is subject to change as you require, as long as you stay true to the principles discussed here.

We have watched Johnny's successes grow from two to six days per week, over a six-week period, impressive change showing that Johnny is benefitting from the approach. Most importantly, we know that if his parents continue to reinforce Johnny's behavior, it is virtually inevitable that he will reach the 100 percent probability of continuing to meet expectations. That is, he will have become responsible for his own behavior by self-reinforcement, achieving mastery free of parental direction and rewards.

Let us go on to consider in a somewhat more structured way how you can get the most out of reviewing your child's chart a few weeks into the program and then periodically thereafter. Over time a variety of circumstances will require you to make modifications in your program. Most of these can be anticipated and will not present major problems.

Respond to Faltering Progress

As you look over each of the items in your child's program (as illustrated above), note any items that seem not to be responding as well as expected or not as well as other items. Anywhere progress seems unduly slow, review how your set up fits with the principles laid out from the beginning, including that each item was written to meet the three basic characteristics of well-worded target behaviors.

1. Check each under-performing item to be sure each is **realistically reachable**, considering what you know about your child. Items showing little or no progress may be too demanding even if you know your child is capable and you have seen the behavior happen. While sheer ability is important, it is also important to consider the past reactions and feelings

MONITOR, MAINTAIN, AND ADJUST YOUR HOME PROGRAM.

about the behavior to assure the standards are set at a level for the child to succeed a third or more of the time.

For any item that might not be set at a realistic level, consider breaking it into parts and assign credits to each part. Remember to praise success for each item as it occurs. As an example, an item may state that:

Jada, you are successful when you are up, dressed, and down for breakfast by 7:30 a.m.

For some children who get most of the steps right without help, this item may be a very useful, prompting them to focus just a bit more and to get everything done on time. But it may be too much for a child who seems to struggle to get up and who eventually appears at the table partially dressed. In such a situation, it might be more constructive to break the item into two or more parts, for example:

Jada, you are successful when you are up by 7:10 a.m.

Jada, you are successful when you are completely dressed and down for breakfast by 7:30 a.m.

While at first Jada may not complete both items successfully, she may be able to do one and, with reinforcement, build on her compliance to complete the second item, improving her chances of overall success.

2. For each item that appears realistically reachable but still shows little or no progress, make sure that it is worded in positive terms, that is, focused on what you do want your child to do, not on what your child should not do. If you discover the words "no" or "not" or "don't," rewrite those items, focusing on the behavior you would like to see that is also directly incompatible with the behavior you'd like to stop.

Even if you find no clearly negative words in the items of concern, look for the insidious word "without," for examples, "without sassing" or "without whining" or "without reminders." Such phrases introduce a negative tone by drawing attention to the very behaviors you are trying to eliminate, and we know that attention itself can be very reinforcing. Reword any such items. For example substitute:

. . .in a respectful way. . . for . . .without sassing. . .,

143

. . .in your ten-year-old voice. . . for . . .without whining. . ., and

. . .on your own. . . for . . .without reminders. . .

Note that even using the word *"if"* for *"when"* in the phrase *"You are successful. . ."* can introduce a negative component. *"If"* suggests doubt that the child will succeed, whereas "when" shows a clear expectation that the child will succeed, if not now, then later. When we have constructed the program correctly, the child **will** succeed.

By going over the first two steps, you will have made sure that all items are realistically reachable for your child and that the target items are positively focused on what you expect your child to do.

3   Review each item of concern again to assess whether the **criteria of success are as clear as possible**. Phrases such as "is good at" or "behaves" provide little clarity for a child. They also offer a child working to gain some sense of control an opportunity to challenge the parents by doing the minimum implied by the vague statement.

Many parents are confident that "My child knows exactly what she is supposed to do," only to discover that what was so clear to them was not at all clear to the child. Often it turns out that even the two parents don't have exactly the same expectations, something recognized only while defining them for their program. Such vagueness can confuse a child but also can allow one to exploit parental inconsistencies. Clearly stating expectations in this program is one aspect that makes it so effective.

As noted earlier, it can be especially challenging to define clear expectations in a school extension of your program. A busy teacher may prefer very general statements of expectations, leaving your child uncertain how to succeed. Be sure to check any school items for clarity.

If you wonder how clear your statements are, ask your child to explain the standard of success for each. Rewrite any that your child can't explain clearly and then explain it again to your child, asking the child to repeat it again. If you have items that don't lend themselves completely to defined standards (e.g., *"gets along with"*), be sure that you handle the dilemma consistently and in a manner that avoids tug-of-wars with your child as described in Chapter 3.

These three steps are designed to help you consider carefully any items in your program that are not showing good progress. Once you have identified needed modifications, rework the relevant items to assure that they are realistically reachable, positive, and clear. That reworking will allow you to continue working day by day, week by week to support your child in assuming ever-greater levels of responsible behavior.

Now that you have completed the assessment using your chart and have made appropriate changes to enhance program effectiveness, you are ready to move on to handling those items that are doing well.

Respond to Ongoing Success

When you have reached a point that your child has shown success on an item for a prolonged period, your next step is to determine whether the behavior is operating independently or still requires external reinforcement. Handle the process of determining that and of responding to the outcome carefully. Handled carelessly, it will teach your child that it is good to fail from time to time in order to keep the goodies coming. Handled well, it will teach the child how good it can feel to master one's own behavior, a splendid gift from you to your child. So, what is required to assure the better outcome?

Assess the record

First review your child's successes on a specific item from start to the present, as we did earlier for the item about Johnny getting the trash out. Use your own judgment as to how rapidly your child is assuming responsibility for each behavior. Some children may reach mastery on some behaviors after just a couple of weeks while on other behaviors only after much longer times. What matters is not the speed but the certainty since you are building a life-time of responsible behavior.

Here is a rule of thumb to guide your next move:

> *When you have seen* ***six weeks of near-perfect performance*** *on an item, it is appropriate to consider checking for internalization of the behavior and possibly fading out your reinforcement.*

Just as we adults sometimes fail to live up to our own standards but still generally manage our responsibilities, children can show occasional lapses as they progress in your program and still be progressing well. Waiting for perfect performance likely would mean that you could never move on.

Fade out reinforcement

When your child's successes appear consistent, prepare for a gradual reduction of reinforcement, a process that will both assess your child's readiness for independence and allow you to reverse course easily should you discover your child still needs reinforcement from you. Your role while fading an item out of your program includes:

- Preparing your child for a change in the frequency or in the amount of reinforcement provided for successful completion of the behavior.
- Implementing a gradual withdrawal or fading of reinforcement for the behavior.
- Making sure that your child recognizes and appreciates the accomplishment involved in achieving mastery of the behavior.

> *The child supplies the power but the parents have to do the steering.*
>
> ~Benjamin Spock, M.D.

Plan to implement your changes during a daily review when you all are relaxed, when you have time to go over the whole situation carefully, and when you can watch your child's reactions. After completing your usual review, identify the item that you think your child may have mastered and comment on it specifically. Point out the successes over the past several weeks on your charts. Then begin the fading process with a comment like:

> *Look, Kai! Your charts show that you have done great at getting the trash out on time for the past six weeks. It looks as if you may not need our help so much anymore!*

Since an alert child, hearing this the first time, may immediately object to what can be perceived as a threat of a loss of benefits, be prepared to calm such worries by going on:

> *We are really proud of your progress. Because you seem to have mastered this job, we are going to change the program a bit. Starting next Monday, instead of ten credits each time you finish the job correctly, you will earn five.*

MONITOR, MAINTAIN, AND ADJUST YOUR HOME PROGRAM.

This comment may further the sense of threat and you may hear, "Hey, that's not fair," so continue your explanation with:

> *But we are also going to make another change because we know that you are eager to earn enough credits for a new bike seat. We have noticed that it is still hard for you to get your math assignment done on time each day, and we want to help you get more used to doing that. We will add the five credits you don't seem to need any more to get the trash out to the ten credits you can already earn to get your math done on time, making it 15 credits in all. That way you can still earn the same number of credits, and we hope this will help with your math, too*

Typically this helps children calm enough to show some interest and at least to listen. Once it is clear the changes will not interfere with chances to earn a prized reward, the child is likely to be more accepting. That, then, allows you to complete this central and hugely important message:

> *Kai, we are really proud of how well you have mastered the job of getting the trash out on your own. Your dad and I have noticed that you also seem proud of yourself for getting this done so quickly each day, and both of us are really happy about that, too!*

Mastery is all-important in a child's life, particularly among children who seem not to show a lot of it. When you tried to help your two-year-old, you likely were rebuked a few times with a haughty *"I can do it myself!"* That is the refrain of a child eagerly pursuing a sense of mastery, something most of us continue to do in a variety of realms for our entire lives.

> *A boy playing a video game shows times when he is frustrated, even fuming at the video screen while still working intensely to progress. Too much of that and he tosses the controller aside and quits for a time. But later he goes back again and again until finally "winning" the game. He may brag and strut briefly and then start all over again, perhaps displaying many of the same reactions, though this time he may be less frustrated as things go better. He may go on to complete the game a number of times, getting better each time before finally putting it in storage once he feels competent and ready to try new challenges.*

If there are no items in your child's chart to which you want to add credits, consider adding a new item instead. Then tell the child that you're going to transfer the credits reduced from the successful behavior to the new one.

By his point you have told the child how your program will be different beginning the next day. And you have calmed any concerns about losing benefits. Next you must follow the new plan faithfully and respond to the child's successes just as you did before, although it is a good idea to increase the amount of your social reinforcement for the first few times:

> *Terrific, Kai, you are doing great at getting the trash out! It is so good to see you doing things so much on your own.*

If your child continues to do well after the reduction in credits, you have evidence that you were right in estimating that you could reduce rewards. After a few more weeks at the new level, you can again use the fading process during a daily review. As before, fade the credits by reducing the number by a reasonable amount, typically half. Explain what you intend to do, and express your pride in the successes that allow for the changes.

With younger children using tokens, for items receiving only one token in the first place, it isn't so obvious how to reduce them, though if you are using tokens that literally can be cut in half you could do that; your child might even enjoy using two halves to make a whole. You may be able to think of other ways to handle this, but some parents have been successful by providing the child with one token for two successes as the first step in fading out the tokens. With these children, give extra praise during the fading process to make up for any sense of loss from fewer tokens. Otherwise, the process is pretty much the same as for older children.

Respond to your child's mastery

For items that start with few credits, only a step or two of fading may bring you to a level where cutting the number further leaves too little to be meaningful. In that case you may move to remove the item entirely.

Reaching this point should be seen as a *big* deal, both because your child has truly accomplished something important and because there is some risk of return to earlier problems when your child recognizes a loss of reward. Make sure that your child fully recognizes that achievement. At your daily review you can emphasize the mastery and can stress how pleased you are. You also can present the child with a special "certificate of mastery" to acknowledge the success. The simple sample shown below was developed on a home computer.

MONITOR, MAINTAIN, AND ADJUST YOUR HOME PROGRAM.

> **Certificate of Mastery**
>
> This is to certify that you
>
> *Jeffrey Sontag*
>
> have successfully mastered
> and
> have assumed responsibility for:
>
> *Keeping our home clean by removing trash from every room in the house in a timely manner*
>
> Recorded this 14th Day of July, 2011
>
> Signed ____*Mom and Dad*____ .

Figure 13. Sample Certificate of Mastery to enhance reinforcement

Manage Lapses in Your Child's Progress

After you reduce reinforcement for a behavior your child had been handling well, if the child does not succeed as often, you may have misjudged the child's readiness. Remain calm and continue your practice of praising successes, stifling any impulse to remark, *"But you had been doing so well!"* Even if your child does not complete the task for a couple days in a row, you need not panic. But if it continues after that, it is time to reverse your changes. Taking this step should not be seen as a failure but simply as evidence that the child wasn't yet ready for the change.

At the end of your daily review very calmly say to the child something like:

> *Well, Kai, I guess we jumped the gun by reducing the credits you earned for getting the trash out on time. We see you still need our help and we have put those five credits back so that now you can earn ten credits just like you did before. We are sorry we made it harder for you, but we know you can get back on track and do as well as you did before.*

But with Kai, we combined five credits taken from getting the trash out with the points he could earn for getting his math assignment in on time. Now

Kai's parents have to make a choice about how to handle the credits, especially if he has shown improvement in math. If they move the credits back to the trash, Kai may lose his progress in math. An alternative is for the parents simply to add five more credits into the system, leaving the moved credits where they were placed. The effect will be to inflate the system just a bit, meaning the child may get to his material reward a bit sooner. Most parents would not find this a problem if they are seeing good results.

When you next feel your child is ready, return to Step 2 to try again.

Adjust Your Program to Changing Circumstances

Fit Your Program to Special Occasions

So far I have discussed adjusting your program to meet changing needs. Some other reasons for making modifications in your program warrant separate discussion.

Special Days

Changes in family routines due to special occasions such as holidays sometimes require program changes. The key is to plan for and make the changes *ahead of time* to avoid later trying to make adjustments in the face of disappointed children unable to follow their programs; as always, it is important to avoid inadvertently reinforcing fussing.

> *On the way to visit grandparents for Thanksgiving, your children in the back seat begin fussing with each other, the conflict growing as the miles pass. You tell them both to stay quiet. This momentarily silences the children, but the din picks up again, with some whining about the long trip and complaints that "she is on my side!" Eventually you react angrily, the children pout, and the trip, meant to be such fun, turns bleak and dark. You might be tempted to try a "fix" by announcing that if the children behave themselves, they can earn a certain number of credits. However, by that point, with irritation in the air, it is likely that the real impact would be to reinforce the earlier conflict rather than the hoped for calm. In the process you might taint the program as a whole.*

Planning ahead can avoid such hassles and set the stage for a pleasant family outing. Anticipate coming changes in your routine that may be challenges to

MONITOR, MAINTAIN, AND ADJUST YOUR HOME PROGRAM.

the children and to you during the atypical circumstances. That will allow you to use your program to avoid problems and reward responsible behavior fitting the situation. For example, to avoid the above conflict-ridden trip, during the family review a day or two before the planned trip, you might say:

> *Children, Thursday is Thanksgiving and your school day items won't apply when we drive to Grandma's for dinner. We know the long drive can be boring and tiring. To help you with the trip, just for tomorrow and for Sunday when we come back, we are going to have a special part in the program. Miranda, for every half-hour you stay calm and pleasant in the car, you will get five credits. And Marky, for each fifteen minutes you stay calm and pleasant, you'll get a token. We know you both can do really well. We are going to have such a good time!*

With a plan and a special chart to track success, your role would be to praise the children for each success. You also would have to improvise a time and place for the daily review while away from home. And, if you so choose, you might modify other aspects of the home program for the days while at Grandma's if you anticipate any other challenges for your children' behavior.

> *There are no seven wonders of the world in the eyes of a child. There are seven million.*
>
> ~Walt Streightiff

Special Seasons

A variation on this sort of change arises during longer alterations in your routine, most commonly with the arrival of school breaks.

Adapt your program to vacation behaviors

Many parents choose to continue their programs through vacation times with suitable modifications to support their overall goal of teaching responsible behavior. If you choose to follow suit, you might reduce expectations just as you may expect less of yourself during vacations. Even then you can maintain focus on the larger picture, supporting your child's maturation as a responsible person. Review your overall program and then continue suitable items, adding others to fit your routine and your expectations during vacation periods.

Assure that your items cover behaviors of interest and are all realistic, positive, and clear, and then assign credits accordingly.

Families who take long vacation trips face special challenges with which your program can be helpful. While such trips typically start filled with anticipation and excitement, the tedium of long hours of restricted activities during travel tends to take its toll. To counter this, bring along suitable activities, books, and games for the children. Where possible, schedule stops to stretch and play along the way, preferably with activities that burn off energy pent up during the long ride. In addition, define age-appropriate target behaviors that will support a pleasant trip. For example:

Lakota (seven years old), you are successful when you draw a picture of something special you see during the day's travel.

Anoki (nine years old), you are successful when you write a half-page description of something special you see during the day.

Awarding credits for completion of such activities benefits children directly, by keeping them busy and by focusing them on what they see along the way.

Consistent with the goal of teaching responsible behavior, you could also include a few items identifying age-appropriate chores so that they each child contributes to family life. For example:

Lakota, you are successful when you carry your toy case into the motel.

Anoki, you are successful when you have your book bag packed and ready to take to the car before we leave for breakfast each day.

Whether you continue the program during vacation periods, though, remains your choice. There is not a right or wrong answer in this matter, but there are opportunities to further your goals if you so choose.

Note that while I focused here on the universal of school vacation, the same concepts apply equally well to any other extended period during which your family might benefit from a modification in your program.

How to take a recess from your program

Parts of your program likely will not apply when school is out. You may choose simply to take a recess from the program. This approach may present no problem as long as you reinstate it when school resumes. Unfortunately, there are several potential risks to this choice. Your child likely has gotten used

MONITOR, MAINTAIN, AND ADJUST YOUR HOME PROGRAM.

to and comfortable with the routine of the program and also is surely focused on a specific reward. If you just suddenly stop the program, the child will feel as if earned credits are really bogus, much as we might if our money suddenly was declared unspendable. Even though you know you will resume the program in a few months, your child, facing a summer of freedom from school, will not want to anticipate the arrival of fall and the end of vacation in order to enjoy benefits of already completed efforts.

To avoid such disappointment, anticipate changes in your routine and prepare suitable modifications. Tell your child what to expect and when to expect it. Also track closely what reward the child is working toward to assure that the chosen goal can be reached by the time you suspend the program. Since it is unlikely that the reward will be earned exactly when you want to stop for vacation, plan ways your child can get to the reward even if it isn't reached by then. For example, you could continue an item or two with enough credits to allow earning the reward. Or you could add a few items specific to vacation just to reach the goal. For instance, if there are a few chores that you might want done one time only, you could offer credits for their completion. Be generous in this regard to assure your child feels good about the program and does not feel cheated by its suspension. This will also help set the stage for when you are ready to resume it in the fall.

As the vacation winds down and resumption of the program nears, plan the steps necessary to restart your program. Decide which target behaviors to include on the chart and which rewards to offer, considering your child's preferences. Reviewing the basics of the program will provide a good guide to this process. Be prepared to start back a few steps from the previous level, since it could take a while for your child to reach the prior levels of performance on any items that you carry over from the earlier program,

How to Discontinue Your Program

While the home program is appropriately used in many families well into adolescence, some parents elect to discontinue their structured programs earlier. Should you choose to do so, here are some guidelines to help you maximize the benefits and minimize the potential negative effects.

To prepare yourself for the necessary steps, recognize that your home program represents an agreement between you and your child about the benefits of behaving responsibly. To eliminate the program from your family life while minimizing the potential detrimental effect on that vital message, plan how to remove the program structure while maintaining your supportive attitude and attention to responsible behavior.

Start by systematically reviewing how your child is doing on each item in your program, as well as the child's progress toward whatever reward is of most interest, to assure you will end without breaking faith with your child.

Once you have a good sense of the status of each item, explain your plans to your child and what you each can expect, stressing your continuing interest in how well the child handles responsibility. Even though you will have gone through the fading process several times, your child likely will not readily accept your plan to reduce the number of items available for earning credits. What follows is intended to help you deal with those concerns.

Fade each item from your chart until your child has achieved mastery for each. Since you will gradually have fewer items in your program, your child will have fewer opportunities to earn credits and will worry about being able to achieve a planned reward. The child may even worry about losing your support. Lessen such concerns by increasing the number of credits for each success, keeping the total close to the original. Over time, as you get down to only a few items, this could become difficult, and you will have to adjust accordingly, finally arriving at the point where no credits are involved.

As you approach this stage, make sure your child will be able to earn enough credits for the final selected reward and won't be left with worthless credits at the end. Be especially generous with supportive social reinforcement throughout this process. Keep in mind that all of these principles will continue to operate in your child and in your home even after you no longer use a structured program to take advantage of them. Therefore, continue to utilize the Principle of Positive Reinforcement even in an unstructured format. Especially avoid slipping back to the all-too-easy pattern of paying more attention to inappropriate behaviors than to those you consider appropriate.

These steps may lessen any negative impact of discontinuing your home program. Should you find your child struggling after the fact, remember that the structured home program offers powerful support for instilling responsible behavior in your child. While you can re-institute it at any time, your child may be wary when you restart it until trust is reestablished.

MONITOR, MAINTAIN, AND ADJUST YOUR HOME PROGRAM.

Troubleshoot Your Program

Even the most successful program may at times show some problems. Fortunately some sleuthing and suitable modifications are likely to get you back on track. As with most problems, those that arise in a home program are more easily resolved by taking action sooner rather than later. One bonus of the daily review is that it keeps you constantly aware of how your child is doing and thus more likely to notice any significant setback early on. Taking calm action as soon as problems are identified will pay long-term benefits.

What follows focuses on families who have had some success followed by signs of decline in their home programs.

Diminishing Benefits of Your Rewards

The most common problems in programs showing initial success but declining effectiveness also turn out to be the easiest to identify and resolve. They most often involve the reinforcement side of the program.

Children who have already earned the most-prized rewards or whose interests have changed are at risk of losing their investment in doing well. To determine whether your child has lost interest in the available rewards, as you complete one of your daily reviews, ask the child something like:

Well, Carlos, what reward are you working toward now? Or

Carlos, are you still working toward that family trip to the park?

A child eager for a specific reward may describe the reward enthusiastically, explaining in detail how much fun it will be and maybe even exactly how many more credits are required to reach the goal. On the other hand, a child whose interests have waned may appear rather vague or unenthusiastic when asked about the reward. To clarify, ask a question like this:

You don't seem very interested in any rewards on our list right now. Is there something you'd like us to consider adding to your reward list?

A child who has lost interest in choices on the list may produce a long list of all the things hoped for but not received on the last birthday. If that happens, you probably have identified the key issue. Your next steps are to:

- Consider choices your child suggests;
- Select those that fit your family's values, resources, and time; and

- Settle on the number of credits required for each new item.

With that done, just monitor the situation for a few days to see if the modification accomplishes what you had hoped. If so, enjoy.

Since some children aren't so eager to suggest new reward choices even if they have lost interest in those on their list, don't assume that a blah response means the problem is elsewhere. Instead try to determine whether there might be new reward choices that will increase your child's interest and motivation to do well on the program. You can address this further with a comment such as:

> *It looks like you can't think of anything special to add right now. Why don't you think about it a bit and when we meet for our daily review Sunday, we'll discuss it again.*

This may be enough to start the wheels turning and encourage your child to think of things to work toward. In a few days you can ask whether the child is considering anything interesting to suggest.

> *It is better to bind your children to you by a feeling of respect and by gentleness, than by fear.*
>
> ~Terence

Meanwhile, you can think about things you know are of interest to your child and plant some seeds or even just directly suggest a specific idea. You are most likely to succeed in this effort if you watch the things the child shows ongoing interest in during the course of routine days. Once you have hit on some ideas, you can explore them with the child in a comment such as:

> *Carlos, we've noticed how much you like to watch sports on TV. Would you like a trip to a ball game with Dad as a choice on your reward list?*

Once the child shows interest in one or more additional choices, the task boils down to working those into the program and proceeding from there as discussed just above.

Inconsistent or Diminishing Follow-through

The second most likely source of decline of effectiveness is in your own inconsistent or decreasing follow through on the basics of the program. Just as

MONITOR, MAINTAIN, AND ADJUST YOUR HOME PROGRAM.

children sometimes fail to follow through, so sometimes do their parents, and it can be an uncomfortable issue to confront by parents who are already burdened with too much to do. The following questions are designed to help you determine what may be contributing to declining performance:

1. Are you remembering to ignore inappropriate behaviors? It is very natural to operate on the "squeaky-wheel principle," readily attending to intrusive inappropriate behaviors while taking for granted and ignoring ongoing success behaviors. Children treated that way quickly learn the value of "squeaking" to meet their needs. Add the stresses of everyday life and a touch of impatience, and things can pretty rapidly deteriorate. If you have allowed yourself to return to old practices of reacting to your child's inappropriate behavior, you can expect the program to lose effectiveness. A child who finds it easier to meet important needs by misbehaving will misbehave more. To correct this pattern, work consistently to withhold your attention from inappropriate behavior.

2. Are you remembering to reinforce your child "on the spot" for successful behaviors? Over time it is appropriate to respond less frequently and less flamboyantly to your child's successes. Still it is important from time to time to praise your child's successes on the spot. For example, when you see your child returning to the house with a just-emptied trash can, you might say:

> *Thank you, Juan. It is so good to see you take responsibility for getting the trash out on time. Your good work sure makes things neater and more pleasant for the whole family.*

You might toss in a warm hug to further enhance the impact. And, by the way, allowing your child to overhear you praising your child to other adults can have a powerful impact.

3. Are you continuing to meet daily to review the entire program and to show the child your continuing commitment to the program? It is easy for busy parents to let routines slip. Allowing that to happen with the daily review, however, can directly undermine your entire home program. You may find it difficult to meet as planned every single day, and an occasional unavoidable omission need not destroy the program. Still, if you get away with one skip and it encourages you to put it off more and more, you may well find the program begins to lose its potency.

Your child may conclude that hard work and success aren't really as important as you first indicated and that maybe the child isn't so important either. Many children, long before starting on a home program, will have learned that one way to be important to parents is to misbehave, and they may resort to that old misbehavior if their constructive actions no longer meet their needs. Solidly building the daily review into your family's daily routine will help avoid this deterioration. The result could be among the most pleasant minutes of the day for your family.

4. Are you making sure the child is able to trade in earned credits as agreed?
Busy parents have to balance a whole lot of demands for their time and attention. Faced with more to do than time will allow, they must choose which things are less critical and can be put off. At a tense time, providing earned rewards to a child might seem less critical, particularly for a child doing well overall. But to a child working hard for a desired reward, delay may seem like a serious breach of contract.

Children will naturally experience any delays beyond those in the contract as unfair. Think how you, as an adult, would feel if your boss were to say on pay day, *"We've been too busy this week to print your paycheck."* And imagine asking when to expect it and being told *"We'll see. . ."* If you have reason to think you have been delaying rewards too long, resolve to make the necessary changes and follow through.

5. Are you getting reinforced for your own efforts to teach your child responsible behavior? The Principle of Positive Reinforcement, the basis for this entire approach, applies to all of us. That means you are much more likely to complete your responsibilities for your child's program if you are reinforced as well.

I hope your child's successes are in themselves rewarding to you. Be aware, though, that over time you may take gains for granted and miss the good feelings you deserve. Regular comparisons of your current status with your status when you started may be helpful. You can also find ways to reward yourself – and your parenting partner, if you have one – for successes with the program.

Asking yourself these five questions likely will identify aspects of a sagging program that can be tweaked to revitalize it. If the answer to any of these questions is "no," rethink your efforts and refocus on how to make the program work. This is a powerful and efficient tool when used appropriately, but, as is true with most things in life that pay dividends, your program requires ongoing attention to the elements that make it that way.

CHAPTER 9

ACTUAL FAMILIES, ACTUAL CHALLENGES

Throughout this book I have described concerns facing parents with whom I have worked in order to illustrate salient concepts and practices. I hope that reviewing the reasoning I applied as a child clinical psychologist to support those parents efforts will enhance your own capacity to think through whatever challenges you confront over the years that you work to guide your children toward responsible adulthood. To support your efforts, here are additional real-life situations, each addressing one of a wide variety of challenging circumstances.

REWARDS OR BRIBERY?

You say it is a good idea to reward children for appropriate behavior. Isn't that just a fancy way to say you should bribe your children?

When I first began my classes, many parents asked this question, but when I began sharing parents' reports that whatever form of punishment they used were largely ineffective, the frequency of the question dropped dramatically. Still, the question persists and deserves comment.

It is instructive to consider Webster's Collegiate Dictionary's definition:

> **Bribery**: *the act or practice of giving, offering, or taking rewards for corrupt practices; the act of paying or receiving a reward for a false judgment or testimony, or for the performance of that which is known to be illegal or unjust. It is applied both to the one who gives and to the one who receives the bribe, but especially to the giver.*

The central element here is payment for doing something corrupt, illegal, or otherwise inappropriate.

Thus, your question implies that there is something vastly inappropriate about rewarding children for doing what they are supposed to do. Yet, reinforcing children for appropriate behavior is much the same as paying adults for their work. As a personal example, when I "do the right thing" by caring for people with whom I work as a psychologist, I am paid for my effort and my time – neither illegal nor, I trust you will agree, inappropriate.

Our program of credits and earned rewards – both material and social – reflects an exchange system long accepted in our society. Thus, in marked contrast to a person rewarding corrupt practices, your home program rewards appropriate behavior and provides loving support for your children's growth and development.

One further point should be stressed: the Principle of Positive Reinforcement, upon which this program is based, exists in nature and is a reflection of the way behavior arises and is modified, whether or not we attend to the fact; it is not something we have imposed on our children or ourselves, it is just the way it is. Our monetary systems represent an implicit, if not typically explicitly acknowledged, implementation of the principle.

LEARNED HELPLESSNESS?

Our daughter never does anything without first saying, "You help me!" What can we do?

Some children display what has been called "learned helplessness," perhaps the case with your child. Any child whose first reaction is *"you help me"* is not feeling at all self-sufficient. Ironically, your daughter appears to be very adept at getting adult help, a sign of considerable interpersonal skill, but since she may not recognize it, it is unlikely to improve her own confidence. Your task, then, is to help your child become – and feel – self-sufficient.

When your daughter was age two or so, she likely reacted to your attempts to help her by announcing, *"I can do it myself!"* Sometimes busy and impatient parents habitually take over tasks that children can do themselves, or they otherwise convey the message that their children are incapable. Whatever may have influenced your daughter's development, she now needs to learn that she is quite capable of doing what you expect of her. Children learn to feel capable by observing themselves successfully complete tasks, a fact that you can rely on as you focus your program on your child's needs.

Clearly and carefully define expectations that you know your child can fulfill a third or more of the time. Given the nature of your concerns, include in each item a phrase such as, *"on your own."* For example:

> *Melinda, you are successful when you have all your toys in the family room picked up on your own by 7:00 p.m.*

> *There are only two lasting bequests we can give our children. One of these is roots; the other wings.*
>
> –Hodding Carter, Jr.

Once you are confident that your expectations are realistic, the next step is to assure that the incentives you have established are adequate and well focused. Make sure your child can rapidly earn enough credits to trade for meaningful rewards, particularly early in the program. Since it appears that for some reason your daughter needs to stay close to you, consider reward choices of special activities with you. Having access to some relatively easy successes will assure she can independently succeed on assigned tasks and earn enough credits to trade for time with you, meeting that need through more independent acts. Working this out will take some of your time, but once you guide your child out of this helpless stance, you may well find that you have actually freed up more of your own time than the program requires.

Your role is to define the target behaviors and to provide the reinforcement. You must avoid directly helping with any task; otherwise you will defeat your immediate and long-term goals. What you can do instead is talk about the way the program will work in your home, emphasizing the great rewards that the child can achieve. With these factors all in place and working for your family, you can anticipate that your child will be on her way to mastery of life's challenges rather than to continued helplessness.

Focus on Self-initiated Responsibility

We can reinforce our child for getting his chores done, but we want him to want to do the right thing, not just do them because he gets something for it. How can the program help with that?

Since I share your goal for your son (and all children) to learn to take full responsibility for his own behavior, the issue is not with the intended outcome but with how to get there. Success with your long-range goal depends upon providing your child direct experience with the benefits of being responsible. Based on natural developmental factors, you can best provide that experience by coupling your son's efforts with material and social reinforcement, continuing long enough that he internalizes the connection and no longer requires external reward. As you operate your program, you will assist your son in moving through three distinct phases of internal satisfaction:

1. At first the child feels good about completing a responsibility only because of the reward received, both material and social, and if this were the end point, your concerns would be well justified.

2. With success over time, the child begins to feel good about succeeding for its own sake, sometimes expressed aloud with comments such as:

    Look, Mom, I got the trash out right when I got home from school, and it only took me two minutes so I can go with the guys to ball practice!

This developmentally more-advanced response reflects the child's growing recognition that other benefits often accompany taking responsibility. This provides an alert parent an opportunity to acknowledge and reinforce the child's gains:

Noah, that's great! It makes me so proud when I see your work is done and I'm so happy to see that you have time with your friends.

3. With still more experience with success, the child moves beyond feeling good about getting a reward and even beyond feeling good about additional benefits from being efficient to feeling good about being a responsible person. A child may show this level with a comment like:

ACTUAL FAMILIES, ACTUAL CHALLENGES

> *Dad, sorry I took so long getting out here, but I saw Mr. Brown was having trouble getting his big trash can to the street so I ran over and helped him. He offered me a dollar for helping him, but I told him I take our trash out all the time and I was happy to help.*

A parent learning of a child progressing to this level can further reinforce what is clearly becoming internalized maturity. For example:

> *Alex, it is wonderful to see how responsible and caring you are becoming. Your pride in your own abilities is a sign that you are really maturing. I know Mr. Brown is impressed, too. You are becoming a very responsible guy and we really are glad for you.*

Your home program provides you a direct way to support the very goal you value, but you must recognize it is a process that takes place over time.

Managing Parental Stress

> *I am a single mother and I am trying hard to make the program work, but sometimes I just get fed up and yell at the children when they get too wild. Then I feel like I've blown it. How can I overcome this problem?*

As you know better than I, many aspects of family life are more burdensome to a single parent than to couples who can share the many tasks involved. It is not surprising that you should occasionally become overwhelmed and find it difficult to maintain your composure in the face of challenging children and with too much to do. I have stressed the importance of consistency and follow-through in dealing with children, and while those are solid guides, they can appear inflexible enough that a two-part restatement may be needed:

> **To the extent that** you consistently avoid responding to inappropriate behavior and consistently provide benefit for appropriate behavior, **to that extent** your child will demonstrate increasingly responsible behavior.

While this is straightforward and accurate, since none of us is at our best all the time, it requires a more moderate corollary:

> When you have gotten off track, **to the extent that** you get back on track, **to that extent** the program will be resumed and the benefits restored.

This guideline allows parents what we must allow our children: to be human and therefore sometimes to fall below our best.

It is usually appropriate to express your honest feelings to your children, but be sure your comments are about the behavior and not hurtful comments about the children themselves.

The most constructive way of dealing with the children is to catch them before their behavior escalates to a "too wild" stage. When you notice the process starting or when you recognize signs that things will get out of hand, clearly and firmly tell the children what changes you expect them to make (don't ask, tell). If they modify their behavior as you instruct them to, a few minutes later go to them and comment on their appropriate behavior (without lecturing about how bad they were before). If they do not change, use time-out.

You are to be commended for trying to make things better for your children and for you in the face of difficult circumstances.

Managing Sibling Conflict

We haven't started a chart, but we are trying hard to do what you said and give attention when our child is cooperative. The problem is that he always seems to be hassling his little brother and sister, and we have to do something! What can we do about that?

Because your efforts to make things better are showing little success, you end up reacting to your son's hassling of his siblings. Each time this occurs you unintentionally provide attention – and possibly a sense of control – to the very behavior you would like to stop. As a result, your son can meet his needs for attention and control without complying with your rules. It would be very difficult for you to reward him enough in your informal approach to demonstrate to him that he can better meet his needs by cooperation.

It is difficult for any parent consistently to ignore inappropriate behavior and to reward appropriate behavior. That is why the structured approach was developed, and I suggest that you take the time to institute such a program, focused on your specific concerns. While it will take you an hour or two to get a program laid out, once it is operational you likely will find that you spend a good deal less time and effort on maintaining it than you do now on dealing with misbehavior – and certainly with a good deal more success.

Finally, once you begin, your program will be much more effective if you use the time-out procedure to deal with any "hassling" that occurs.

Actual Families, Actual Challenges

Differing Parental Expectations

My wife and I are disagree about what to put into our program. She says I expect too much from the children, and I think she's too soft. How can we get past this problem?

Many parents operate similarly and over time their expectations and interactions with their children actually grow further and further apart. Each parent, consciously or unconsciously, tries to compensate for supposed errors in the other's style. Most often, as in your case, the mother is seen as "too soft" and the father becomes more demanding to compensate; in response the mother strives to soften the impact of the father's stance, setting up a pattern that feeds on itself even to the point of destroying the family.

Often parents haven't discussed their goals and don't know that they actually both want what is best for their children. To clarify where you each stand on child rearing, find a calm and unhurried time to discuss what you each are hoping to accomplish. Parents who see themselves as far apart on child rearing frequently discover that they actually have pretty much the same goals for their children. Virtually all parents, in one way or another, say they want to raise responsible, hard-working, caring, and even-tempered children. The issue, then, comes down to the best way to reach those goals.

If you are like most couples, the approach discussed in this book is different from what either of you has done before and it therefore represents a kind of neutral ground from which you can start fresh. Your home program invites your child to comply with your expectation with a promise of reward for compliance. Under these circumstances, your "soft" wife need not worry so much about you being too harsh since the child will either succeed or not and will either be rewarded or not – without harsh recrimination for "not."

> *When my kids become wild and unruly, I use a nice, safe playpen. When they're finished, I climb out.*
>
> ~Erma Bombeck

Similarly, the program will directly show how realistic your expectations are based on your child's success rate. If you have set expectations too low, you'll see lots of success and will be able to raise your expectations as each behavior is mastered. If your expectations are too high, your child will rarely succeed, and you'll know that you must reduce the standards to a level that will show success. Working in this fashion will help you find a happy middle ground where you can pool your resources and work together to meet your overall goals for your child. The child's success in assuming responsibility for his or her own behavior will be well worth your efforts.

When Saying "No" is too Difficult

It is just so hard for me to tell my children "no" when they want to do things that I think they shouldn't, and then we end up in fights. How can I get past this?

Quite a few parents these days describe difficulties setting limits on their children and much turmoil in the family as a result. While children often participate actively in intense conflict, almost none like the interactions. Imagine your child asking for something that you decide, after thinking it over, is not appropriate and you say "no." Then picture these two scenarios:

1   Your children object, you repeat your decision, the children whine and complain, you say "no" again, they whine more, you get upset and yell, and the escalation continues until finally you give in – and you all know you will soon repeat the pattern with the same outcome. In this scenario, your children can pretty much count on getting their way, but only after much conflict and unhappiness in your home.

2   Your children object but you have carefully considered the request and you explain your decision one more time, then silently refuse to react to escalating whining, no matter how persistent. While disappointed, the children finally realize there is no point in continuing and the fussing dies away. In this scenario, sometimes the children don't get their way but much more of the time the family is calm and interactions are pleasant.

Now imagine that your children could fully appreciate the differences in the two outcomes. Which reaction do you suppose your children would prefer? I don't know your children but I'd guess they would opt for number 2, fewer fights and more comfort at home even if it means not getting their way sometimes. The problem is that children cannot fully understand such choices and therefore it is up to adults to teach them.

Teenagers, even some labeled "incorrigible," sometimes tell their psychotherapists that "I wish my parents had cared enough for me to stop me." Such a comment is powerful evidence that children need the safety and protection provided by parents who set reasonable limits. It might be useful for you to reread the portion of Chapter 3 about what causes and how to deal with control struggles between parents and children.

Your question, of course, shows that you already realize that you should be able to say "no" and make it stick. This book presents an approach that relies on parents' guiding and supporting children in taking responsibility for their own behavior. Design a program for each of your children, including behavior items related to your concerns. Be sure that you address those situations that have typically led to the conflicts that you described. By defining success behaviors that focus on what you *do* want each child to do – and which are incompatible with the behaviors you want to end – you can expect fewer conflicts when you set limits. Your most loving and helpful gift to your children is the benefit of your greater life experience, including establishing suitable boundaries for them.

When Your Child "Quits" the Program

We were doing pretty well with our program for a few weeks but then our twelve-year-old daughter got very upset. When she left time-out and came to the kitchen, she dropped a pile of tiny scraps of paper on the counter. She announced angrily, "there's your stupid program." The pieces were her chart. Since she destroyed the program, what do we do now?

Your daughter surely let you know how she feels, or at least how she felt when she tore up the chart. Somehow she managed to construe the program into something punitive. It may be scary for her now that you are operating differently. Perhaps before she felt confident about how to meet her needs, and now she isn't so sure. Or maybe now it looks to her as though she has to exert more effort to get what she got before with less effort.

When your daughter gave you the torn up chart and told you it was "your stupid program," you accepted that she had "destroyed the program." But only if you agree that the chart *is* the program would that be true. My view is that the chart is a tool for keeping track of the program, but it is not the program itself. You can best think of the program as consisting of your expectations for your child and your manner of assuring your daughter meets them. If loss of the chart makes you change your expectations or makes you give up your commitment to dealing with her by reinforcing what you expect from her, then she will have, in fact, destroyed the program.

That choice, however, is not hers but yours.

How, then, might you best react to this turn of events? The first step, I would suggest, is sitting down with your daughter when she is calm and telling her that you realize that she was upset when she tore up the chart and asking her to help you understand what was bothering her. Then try to listen only, without defending yourself or explaining away whatever she says. You may learn that the chart and program had nothing to do with the reaction, and if so, you can discuss the concern separately and determine a suitable response.

Some concerns may even lend themselves to inclusion within the program. Suppose, for example, that her complaint was that her younger brother was getting all your attention because he was earning so many credits on his own program. After acknowledging that it must be frustrating to watch, you could offer to review her program and determine whether some of the items might be modified to allow her more successes herself.

But suppose all you learn is that your daughter finds the program unduly demanding since she had things her own way prior to its start. Your task at that point would be to make it clear that the program is still in effect and that neither your expectations nor your manner of dealing with them has changed.

Since the chart was torn up, you will have to make a new one, and that presents a problem since you are unlikely to remember each of the child's successes from the beginning of the chart. I suggest that you do the best you can to reconstruct the credits earned, discussing it with your daughter if you can do so calmly. I would not suggest that you let her tell you which points she earned, since that would tempt her to fudge, but rather that you have her tell you things that can jog your own memory. For example, she might say:

> *Remember, Mom, that I vacuumed the living room right after I got home from Mary's that day, and you told me how good it was that I did it before you set up for your book club.*

If your child is too angry to participate, do the best you can and tell her that you are sorry that there may be some errors that you can't fix because of the circumstances. I urge you not to turn this into a lecture since doing so is unlikely to convey anything she doesn't already realize, but it could end up giving undue attention to negatives. If she complains about credits she thinks she should have but you aren't sure about, explain why you can't include them, and to further complaining, say:

> *I'm sorry if you don't' understand. I've reconstructed as much of the chart as I can and I've explained it the best I can, and that's just the way it is.*

From then on, do not participate further in discussion since doing so would only continue a fruitless process.

If your daughter is really upset about the program, she may still tell you angrily, *"I'm just not going to do the program again, and I don't care what you say!"* It will be good to anticipate such a reaction so that you are ready with your own response. At that moment explain, *"I'm sorry you feel that way, but the program is the way we are doing things in our home now."* Whatever retorts or protests you hear, just disengage.

> *The trouble with having a stubbornness contest with your kids is that they have your stubbornness gene.*
>
> ~Robert Brault

From then on continue to operate as I have discussed. Even a child who is determined not to cooperate is likely to complete some expectation on your target behavior list, and when she does, be sure to offer appropriate praise, neither overly effusive, nor sarcastic, nor blah. This may be difficult for you if your daughter has been sulky and unpleasant for some time, but it will pay big dividends for you to demonstrate that the program continues to work exactly as you said it would.

In some measure, your child is testing whether you really mean to reward the behaviors in the program while withholding response to inappropriate ones. Passing the test will require you to maintain your own discipline and thereby model the very things you mean to teach: responsibility for one's own behavior. In the process you will demonstrate to your daughter that she will continue to benefit whenever she meets your expectations. At some point, she is likely to become interested in the rewards on your list. When that happens, reward yourself as well since you will have faced about as tough a challenge to the program as anyone is likely to.

One more note: since you started by saying that you were doing rather well with the program for a couple of weeks, I am assuming your target behaviors are realistically reachable, positive, and clearly stated. Still, it could be useful to review each item to be sure since poorly written items could contribute to your daughter's upset. Making adjustments according to your review could be part of your response to her if you find things that bear improvement.

Assisting a Child with Attention Deficit Disorder

We have carefully considered all you have said and wished it would work for us, but our son has ADD. His medication is helping him some, but he still has a hard time controlling himself, especially on weekends when his doctor said it is good for him not to take his pills. Is there any way this approach can help in our situation?

Children with Attention Deficit Disorder present enormous challenges to their parents and teachers, as illustrated in this anecdote:

> *Nine-year-old Dirk was referred by his pediatrician and brought in by his parents. He had been on medication for years for hyperactivity and distractibility, hallmarks of ADD. Dirk's behavior problems had escalated both at home and school despite several increases in dosage over the last couple of years and the pediatrician was reluctant to increase it again.*
>
> *To be sure I wouldn't miss important details, I took notes as the parents enumerated their many concerns about this boy. Dirk, meanwhile, roamed my office, displaying many of the behaviors his parents were telling me occurred regularly at home and school. He poked through the toys but played with none, pushed and pulled at books on the shelves, crawled behind the desk, fiddled with the curtains, and generally was unfocused and constantly active.*
>
> *After half an hour, the parents left and I met with Dirk alone. Asked why they had come to see me, he said that he didn't know. Asked what his parents had told me, again he said he didn't know, and he continued to squirm and wiggle, occasionally slithering out of the chair that I'd asked him to sit in while we talked. After a time, I told him I could see it was difficult for him to remember what we had talked about and that I was going to help. I drew a star on a piece of paper with a red marker and told him that for each one of his parents' concerns that he could tell me, I would draw him a star.*
>
> *Dirk said that he hadn't been listening and thus didn't know. With some urging, he finally mumbled vaguely about something his parents had mentioned, and I quickly drew a star on the paper as he watched. Again he insisted that he couldn't tell me anything else, but with more urging, he came up with another concern, this time in richer detail. As*

ACTUAL FAMILIES, ACTUAL CHALLENGES

I drew his second star, I commented that we had just gotten started and already he had thought of two things. By then the boy was sitting in his chair and seemed interested although still asserting he couldn't think of anything. But more quickly, he added another of his parents' concerns and before I had drawn his third star, he was telling me of another. I won't continue with each step, but by the time we were done, he had mentioned all but one or two of the rather long list of concerns I had written in my notes, and he had nearly a dozen stars on his paper. More impressive still, he sat in his chair looking stunned – but excited – as he considered his stars and exclaimed, "Wow! I can't believe I remembered all those things."

As the parents returned to the office, Dirk jumped up and thrust his sheet of stars at them. He told them excitedly that he had been able to tell me almost everything they had said about his problems, adding at the end, "And I didn't think I was even listening." Initially the parents reacted to Dirk's excited outburst as typical for Dirk. Still, when the boy sat back down in his chair, they did seem to notice. I asked him then to tell them some of the things he had told me, and he rattled off several of the items in a remarkably organized and clear fashion, running his finger down the row of stars as if ticking them off as he spoke. His parents listened in apparent disbelief and then turned to me for comment. I further described what happened, noting that the boy had displayed internal resources that seemed at odds with his history.

To make a long story manageable, we spent another half hour or so together, building on the experience in the office by designing a simple reward program. Our intention was to support this boy's success in focusing his attention and maintaining appropriate control over his behavior in key situations at home with a simple addition for school. The parents, themselves, clearly as stunned as they were hopeful, asked about the medication. I urged them to wait until we could determine how their son managed with the new behavior checklist, and then we could communicate with the pediatrician about what might be best to do.

A couple of weeks later, the family returned with the charts from their program, all three regaling me with stories about how well Dirk had been doing, all clearly reflected in the data from their charts.

As this second meeting ended, I suggested that the parents talk to the pediatrician, hopeful that he would agree there was no reason to raise

> *the dosage. I was startled to learn that the parents had chosen to discontinue the medication on their own only a couple of days after our initial visit, not something I would have recommend. Still, in this case the boy had been medication-free for ten days without complications and the successes they described actually occurred without benefit of medication.*
>
> *It seemed clear to me that the most important change in this situation came about because of this boy's markedly altered view of himself. He went from seeing himself as incapable of noticing anything or of containing his own squirminess to announcing that he had, and could, tell me most of what his parents had said, a change that carried over long after they left my office.*

So what is the point of this anecdote? While I share concerns that medication may be overused in some children, clearly there are children for whom medication provides essential support for their capacity to deal constructively with a world that otherwise is overwhelming and discouraging. Thus, it is not my intention to suggest that all children should be taken off medication and put on a home program and surely not without consulting the child's doctor.

Nor do I have any illusions that our simple program overcame this boy's attention and behavior control problems. I think it is likely that for some unknown reason his nervous system had matured beyond his need for medication. But because he had already come to see himself as a "hyper" kid who couldn't be expected to control himself, he lived accordingly. Once he discovered this was no longer true, he was able to refocus his internal resources and function much more effectively.

> *A characteristic of the normal child is he doesn't act that way very often.*
>
> -Author Unknown

But what about the many children with this condition who may or may not benefit from medication and who are still struggling to fit in at home and school? Every child must learn to function adequately in the world with whatever demands and expectations that entails. Because children with attention and control struggles typically have a more difficult time meeting expectations, they are in special need of help in focusing their behavior.

The approach described in this book is especially well suited to provide that focus. By carefully defining realistically reachable expectations put in positive terms, by providing meaningful incentives for meeting those expectations, and by consistently managing the connections among the elements of a home program, parents of such children can support continuing maturation toward effective behavior control and – ultimately – self-responsibility.

My answer to you, then, is that the approach presented here might be very well suited to your needs. Your challenge will be carefully to design a program *to meet your son where he is,* to support his moves toward better self control, and to nurture his awareness of his progress as it occurs so that he fully appreciates his own capacities. The only aspect of your challenge that might seem specific to ADD is that extra care may be required to assure your target behaviors are in small enough steps for your child to succeed. Thus, an appropriate item for a child without ADD might be:

> *Conrad, you are successful when you complete your math problems during study period.*

A child with ADD, on the other hand, may require several less demanding items to cover the same basic task:

> *Albert, you are successful when you stay at your desk for ten minutes,*
>
> *Albert, you are successful when you write your assignment on your daily log, and*
>
> *Albert, you are successful when you complete five math problems during study period.*

As you can see, I have emphasized for you the importance of special care in defining target behaviors – specifically to assure that each item you include is truly realistically reachable for your son in the light of his extra struggle to stay focused. Chosen carefully, the successes for those items, however small at first, can be the foundation for continuing growth for you both.

Your Program and Children of Divorce

This program sounds like it might be a good idea, but I am divorced and my children' father won't go along with any of it, so what can I do?

Many single parents report similar struggles and are concerned about how the program can work for them. Of course, it is better if parents can agree on exactly how to raise their children, but even in intact homes, perfect agreement is often not the case. Actually, it may be at least somewhat easier to deal with children in a home where you have complete control than in one where you and the other parent disagree strongly about discipline.

The keys in this situation are not unique: make it clear to your children what is expected, avoid supplying benefit for inappropriate behavior, and meet their important needs when your children are doing what is expected.

You may be worried that your children will be confused if the expectations aren't the same in both households. But it is not essential that you and the children's father have the same expectations or use the same approach. Note that by three years of age many children are in preschool where they quickly learn that expectations are different in school than they are at home. In school they learn that they must take turns with other children, that they must stay quiet during nap-time, that they must share, and that they must follow other adults' instructions. Most children, after a brief period of adjustment, have no trouble going from their home, with its set of expectations, to school, with its different expectations, and back to home again. Further, within the school day, they learn they can be quite boisterous on the playground but must suddenly be much more controlled in the classroom. The transition from one parent's home to the other typically demands much less adaptation than do moves from home to school or playground to classroom.

Develop your program to fulfill your goals for your children and follow through accordingly. Your children may complain that your rules are unfair and if you react defensively to the complaint, your children may respond with more complaints. A better response will be to acknowledge there are differences that can be confusing to them. Then calmly reiterate that in your home you do things the way you have laid them out. Of course if there are residual strong negative feelings between you and the father, being calm may be difficult, but it is important that you keep those feelings out of interchanges with your children, who are not responsible for the other parent.

My 12-year-old son returns from a weekend at his dad's house all wound up. When I try to discipline him, he tells me I am mean and says he likes it better with his dad. I then feel bad and it is hard to stick to the program.

It is entirely appropriate for you to have different expectations for your child in your home and to provide the guidance that your child needs in order to meet them successfully. Since you cannot control the practices at the other parent's house, much as you might like to, your effort is better spent on making things work in your home. To reassure yourself that your expectations are suitable, I'd suggest that you start by considering whether your target behaviors are reasonable and appropriate for your son and are in his best interest. If you decide they are not, take time to make suitable revisions until you are satisfied. The structure of the program will guide you through the steps to define exactly what you want to focus on in teaching your child responsible behavior.

When you are confident that your expectations are appropriate, stick to them, knowing that working to achieve them is the most loving thing you can do as a parent – though that may or may not make you a popular parent at any given moment. With that assurance, you can be ready to deal with your child's return from his dad's house.

The transition from his dad's to your house may be a particularly trying time for your son. For example, if he has had a fun weekend with few responsibilities, settling into the routine at your home may not be easy, a bit like returning to work after vacations for us adults. Recognizing this allows you to plan ahead and prepare both of you for the transition. A day or two before your son is to leave, find a calm time to tell him something like this:

> *Zach, you'll be going to your dad's Friday night for the weekend. I know you are really looking forward to it. I'll miss you a lot but I hope you'll have a great time. Sometimes when you come home you are still excited about the neat things you did with your dad. That can make it hard to come back here and get ready for a regular school week. That's kind of the same way I feel each week about going back to work, but we each have to adjust and get ready for what comes next . . .*

This comment is to focus you both on the coming separation and the on return to follow and to acknowledge that the latter is not easy for either of you. Then, in keeping with our overall approach, continue:

> *. . . Since coming back and getting ready for school and your other responsibilities is rather hard for you, I am going to help you. I always look forward to your coming home, and I want us both to be able to enjoy it. So, starting this weekend, you'll have a new item in your program:*

> *Zach, you are successful when you go to your room, unpack your backpack, and have your things put away within thirty minutes after getting home.*

I want us to have time for hugs and for you to tell me a bit about your weekend. But within fifteen minutes, you are to go to your room to unpack and put your things away. That will give you a few minutes of quiet time so that you can feel calmer inside and also get things organized for the coming week. When you are done, we can have a bit more time together and maybe share a treat before bedtime.

Finally, if your child is anticipating something special during the week with you, discussing it could help bridge the transition to life back with you.

The specifics of this are up to you, but the idea is to set up a bit of routine in your home designed to assist in the transition, recognizing that some quiet time alone, along with getting organized a bit for the routine, can be helpful. Keeping everything focused on making things better for you and the child will also set a warm, constructive tone.

A Program for Parents, Too

You have said that all of the principles apply to everyone. Could we somehow set up the same sort of program for my wife and me so that the children will see that we are all in it together?

Yes, the principles apply to adults as well as children. The basics of building a program for yourselves are exactly the same as those for building a program for a child.

You will need to develop a set of relevant target behaviors. Take care to assure each item is realistically reachable, is put in positive terms, and is clearly defined. Then you will need to assign some sort of credits to each item and to develop a list of rewards from which you can select items as you accumulate sufficient credits. And you will need to set aside a time each day to review your progress in the fashion described in this book, perhaps at the same time you review your children's progress. The one complication in applying this approach to yourselves is that you will have to find a way to reward yourselves. If you and your wife were each to set up a program and agree to reinforce each other, you could have a very viable and effective program, the reward side limited only by your creativity.

In keeping with the focus of this book, you might want to include a few items in support of maintaining your children's programs, such as consistently holding your daily reviews and assuring rewards are provided when earned.

Generally, though, the final nature of your own program, as those for your children, depends on your own creativity and effort. I wish you well.

Where did we ever get the crazy idea that in order to make children do better, first we have to make them feel worse? Think of the last time you felt humiliated or treated unfairly. Did you feel like cooperating or doing better?

~Jane Nelson

Appendices

Appendix 1. Identify Target Behaviors

Appendix 2. Blank Home Program Chart

Appendix 3. Sample Prize Game Board - Pre-reading Age Child

HOW TO RAISE DISCIPLINED AND HAPPY CHILDREN

If I had my child to raise all over again,
I'd build self-esteem first, and the house later.
I'd finger-paint more, and point the finger less.
I would do less correcting and more connecting.
I'd take my eyes off my watch, and watch with my eyes.
I'd take more hikes and fly more kites.
Id' stop playing serious, and seriously play.
I would run through more fields and gaze at more stars.
I'd do more hugging and less tugging.

~Diane Loomans

Appendix 1

IDENTIFY TARGET BEHAVIORS

Our goal in this discussion is to assist you in teaching your child better control over his own actions, and a better sense of adequacy in dealing with his world. Once you have read the section dealing with the reasoning behind our approach, you will be ready to design a specific program for use in your own home, based on the changes you would like to help your child make.

The first step is for you to spend some time considering exactly what you hope to accomplish. We have found that the easiest and most effective way to think about the specific behaviors you would like to change is to focus your attention on a typical day in your home. Consider each part of the day, and the tasks typically required of the child during each time period. Then record each behavior you think of which occurs often enough to bother or concern you, or to interfere with your child's comfort in life.

On the attached sheet are listed the typical portions of the day, and some of the tasks associated with each; parents often have identified problems related to these tasks. This is meant only as a guide to your thinking, and not all parts will apply to you and your child. Feel free to add or ignore tasks.

For each issue you think of, write a brief description next to the specific task and the portion of the day during which it is most likely to occur. For example, for "After school: coming home," one parent wrote "often misses bus." Another wrote, "Forgets his lunch pail at least twice a week."

When you have finished going through the list, please check how complete you have been by asking yourself this:

"If my child changes all of the things I've written down, will there still be significant problems?"

If the answer is "yes," think about what else is of concern to you, then add the new issues to your list. Then ask yourself the same question again. When you can comfortably answer "no" you will likely have identified all the behaviors you might want to include in your program. You will deserve to feel pleased that you have done a complete job! This success will make it easier for you to think through how you might design your program as we continue our discussion.

Please keep your completed form at hand while you continue reading. Note that this form is for your use, so use it as a reference as you read, and for use in developing your own program after that.

Please note that we recognize that our approach emphasizes the importance of stating to your child, in clear and positive terms, what you want them to do, rather than drawing all attention to the behaviors you would like to reduce or eliminate. This may seem to be in conflict with the focus of this form, which asks you to identify behaviors of concern to you. The reason for this apparent discrepancy is that most people seem to find it easier to start by listing things that don't work well.

As you progress through reading the details of this approach, you will learn why it is so important to focus on success behaviors, as well as how to most effectively modify your target behavior statements to specify what you do want your child to do.

Identify Target Behaviors

Child's name _____ Date _____

PORTION OF THE DAY/TASKS	ISSUES IN CHILD'S BEHAVIOR
--- Before school ----	
Getting up	
Getting dressed	
Cleaning up (hair, teeth, etc.)	
Eating breakfast	
Getting off to school	
Other (specify _____)	
--- At school ----	
Doing assignments	
Playing on playground	
Cooperating with teacher	
Getting along with peers	
Eating lunch	
Other (specify _____)	
---- After school ----	
Coming home	
Changing clothes	
Doing household chores	
Taking a nap	
Eating dinner	
Doing homework	
Other (specify _____)	

PORTION OF THE DAY/TASKS	ISSUES IN CHILD'S BEHAVIOR
— After dinner ----	
Doing evening chores	
Getting along with family	
Taking a bath	
Putting toys away	
Going to bed	
Other (specify _____)	
---- Anytime/miscellaneous ----	
Cooperating in the car	
Playing independently	
Getting along with siblings	
Cooperating at a store	
Cooperating with parents	
Other (specify _____)	
Other (specify _____)	

Thank you for your effort in completing this task.

Appendix 2

Blank Home Behavior Chart

(For copying or use as a model)

Home Behavior Program

_____, you are successful when: for the week of ____20____

Target behavior	Cred	Mon	Tue	Wed	Thu	Fri	Sat	Sun
1.								
2.								
3.								
4.								
5.								
6.								
7.								
8.								
9.								
10.								
Total daily credits earned								
Credits used								
Running balance								

Appendix 3

Sample Prize Game Board – Pre-Reading Age Child

Below is a sample game board, intended for use with a youngster who can't yet read or count reliably. Most little kids have played on game boards so will recognize the overall idea. Design your own board in similar fashion, drawing or pasting simple pictures representing prize choices on the board to show how many tokens are required for each. Demonstrate placing one token on each step, beginning at "Start," to show how close to each reward you child has come. For example, on the sample board, it takes ten tokens to trade for ice cream. Also show your child that any extra tokens provides a start to the next reward choice.

HOW TO RAISE DISCIPLINED AND HAPPY CHILDREN

INDEX

Age differences, *43-45, 54, 57, 63-65, 71-73, 83*
Anger in parents, 2, 6, *41, 127*
Assign credits for success, *56-58*
Away from home, *123-134, 151, 159*

Basic principle, *x, 25-29*
Basic rationale, *32*
Behavior chart, *65-68, 186*

Car behavior, *130-133*
Chart, behavior, *65-68, 186*
Childhood fears, worries, *14-29*
Consequences of behavior, *10*
Control struggles, *21-28*
    How control struggles arise, *21-24*
    How the process works, *24*
    Possible resolutions, *26-28*
Credits
    Assign credits *56-58*
    Provide meaningful rewards, *59-63*
    Trading credits, 56-65, 89, 93, 158
Criteria of success, *46-52, 100, 144*

Daily review, *68-74, 95, 105, 157*
    Age considerations, *71-73*
    Sample scenario, *69-74*
Define target behaviors, *39-56*
    Clear criteria of success, *46*
    Format: A... is successful when..., *39*
    Realistically reachable goals, *40-45*
    When these are in conflict, *47-52*
    Word goal statements positively, *45*
Developmental factors, *x, 18, 21-23, 161*
Dining out, behavior during, *127-129*
Discipline defined, *11*

Discipline, approaches to, *2-7*
Driving, car behavior, *130-133*

Eating, problems at meal times, *83-87*
Eliminate misbehavior, *23-25, 29-32, 45-48, 107-135*

Family schedule changes, *68, 95*
Fines for failures, *98*

Goal of this book, *x-xiii*
Goal setting, *19, 32, 35-55, 100*
Guideline: avoid haggling, *49-52*
Guideline: positive interaction, *49*
Guideline: When off track, *163*

Home program, elements, *35-74*
    Clear criteria of success, *46-52*
    Positive goal statements, *45*
    Realistically reachable goals, *40-45*
    When these are in conflict, *47-52*
Home program, specify goals, *43-56*
    Define target behaviors, *35-56*
    Format for statements, *39*
    Identify behaviors for focus, *36-38*
Home program, goal statements, *43-56*
    For older kids, *44*
    For younger kids, *44*
    Time factors, when to be done, *42*

Identify behaviors of concern, *36-38*
Illustrative examples
    Attention Deficit Disorder, *170-173*
    Better at dad's house, *174-176*
    Blaming, *78, 121*
    Bribery, *159*
    Car seat, *134*

INDEX

Chores, *82, 162*
Complicated family schedules, *103*
Differing parental expectations, *165*
Diminished interest in reward, *87, 93*
Divorce, conflicting styles, *173*
Establishing a reward system, *87-94*
"Fining" misbehavior, *98*
Helpless child, *160*
Insulting comments, *122*
Kids bickering, *41, 77, 84-6, 121*
Managing a home program, *95-98*
Managing rewards: two kids, *191-193*
Messy room, *75*
Money for rewards?, *90*
"No" – setting limits, *166*
Parental stress, *163*
Pestering, *78*
Picky eaters, *83-87*
Reminders, constantly needed, *82*
Self-esteem, *78-80*
Self-initiated responsibility, *172-173*
Shyness, *78-80*
Sibling conflict, *164*
Single mother, *163*
Slowness, *80-82*
Specifying expectations, *75-86*
Talk on the phone, *76*
Tantrums, *114, 120*
Time-out challenges, *117-122*
Unfair chores, *82*
When your child "quits," *167-169*
When "no" is too difficult, *166*
Whining, *118, 150*
Influence away from child, *99-105*
Internally reinforced behavior, *28*

Mastery of behavior, *vii, 138, 142-149*
Meal time problems, *83-87*

Modifications over time, *137-158*
  Changing circumstance, *150-154*
  Discontinuing the program, *153*
  "Fading" reinforcement, *146-149*
  Final steps to child's mastery, *148*
  Special occasions, *150-153*
  Troubleshoot the program, *155-158*
  When progress falters, *149*
  When success is ongoing, *145-150*
  When things don't go well, *149*
Money rewards, *98-100*
Monitor progress, *137-158*

Natural developmental sequence, *21-23*

Operating procedures, *65-74, 103-105*
  Behavior chart, *65-68, 102-105, 139-141*
  Daily review, *68-74, 95, 105, 139-141, 146-152, 155-158, 167*

Parent survey, *2-4*
Parental anger, *2, 6, 41, 127*
Physical approaches, *2, 16, 32*
Positive attention, *39-40, 86, 133*
Power struggles, *21-28*
  How control struggles arise, *21-24*
  How the process works, *24*
  Possible resolutions, *26-28*
Practice makes permanent, *34*
Principle of positive reinforcement, *2, 33-41, 147. 170*
Probability scale, *35-40*
Provide reward choices, *67-73*
Punishment, impact of, *10-14, 28, 116*

Realistically reachable expectations, *48-53, 55-56, 108, 150-152*
Redeeming "credits" and tokens, *54-65, 83, 89, 93, 158, 187*

INDEX

Reduce misbehavior, *23-25, 29-32, 45-48, 107-135*
Reinforcement, practical issue
    Age factors, *65-67*
    Constraints on delivering, *69*
    Family values, *69*
    Maintaining child's interest, *70*
    Parental financial resources, *68*
    Parental time limitations, *68*
    Special time together, *70*
Reinforcement, types, *29-31*
    Internal reinforcement, *30-31*
    Material reinforcement, *29*
    Social reinforcement, *29*
Reminders, *80, 90, 151*
Replace unwanted behavior, *37-40*
    Directly incompatible, *38-40*
    The bad news, *37*
    The good news, *37-40*
Restrictive approaches, *8*
Reviewing your progress, *146-149*
    A look at your charts, *147-149*
    Your impressions, *146*
Rewards (see "reinforcement")
Resolving power struggles, *26-28*
Rules of thumb
    Goal setting level, *50*
    Number of target items, *47*
    Number of reward choices, *70*
    Telling a child to "stop", *117*
    When to fade out rewards, *153*

Sample materials
    Blank chart, *195*
    Completed charts, *75, 76*
    Identifying target behaviors, *45, 192*
    Mastery certificate, *157*
    Progress across weeks, *148*
    Reward lists, *72, 73*
    School chart, *110*
    Target behavior list, *61, 63*
    Teenager contract, *81*
    Young child game-board, *196*

School behavior extension, *107-113*
    Behavior chart, *109*
    Sett up a school program, *107-113*
Self-esteem, 4, 86-88, 121
Single mothers, *173*
Spanking, *2, 16, 32*
Special occasions, *150-153*
    Considering a "recess," *152*
    Special days, *150*
    Special seasons, *151*
    Vacation modifications, *151*
Structured home program, *35-74*
Summary of the basic rationale, *32*
Supermarket, behavior at, *123-126*

Target behaviors, establishing, *35-55*
    Define target behaviors, *40-47*
    Format goal statements, *39*
    Identify behaviors of concern, *36-39*
Target behaviors (see Writing)
Time-out, away from home, *123-135*
    At a sit-down restaurant, *127-130*
    In the car, *130-135*
    While shopping, *123-126*
Time-out, background, *115*
    Compared to usual approaches, *121*
    Concept, *107-113*
    Elements of success, *113*
    Follow through, *116*
    Manage the end of time-out, *115*
    Prototype of the technique, *112*
    Place for time-out, *111*
    Procedure, *109*
    Purpose, *108*
    The test, *109*
    The time in time-out, *112*
    Time-out with two children, *112*
    Set up, *110*
Time together, *62, 65*
Tokens, *44, 54-64*
Trading "credits" and tokens, *54-65, 83, 89, 93, 158, 187*

INDEX

Troubleshoot your program, *155-158*
    Diminishing benefits of rewards, *155*
    Inconsistent follow through, *156-158*
Turn yourself on "robot," *51, 81, 117, 122, 126, 133*

Verbal approaches, *2*

Ways children learn, *8-10*
    Consequences of behavior, *10*
    Correcting errors, *9*
    Direct instruction, *8*
    Modeling, *9*
Writing target behaviors, *39-56*
    Clear criteria of success, *46*
    Format: "... is successful when...", *39*
    Realistically reachable goals, *40-45*
    When these are in conflict, *47-52*
    Word goal statements positively, *45*

Made in the USA
Charleston, SC
05 June 2011